Playing, Learning and Living

Playing, Learning and Living

VERA ROBERTS

A & C BLACK LTD · LONDON

First published 1971 Reprinted 1972
A. & C. Black Ltd.
4, 5 & 6 Soho Square London WIV 6AD
© 1971 Vera Roberts

ISBN 0 7136 1194 4

Printed in Great Britain by
C. Tinling & Co. Ltd.,
London and Prescot

Contents

Preface   vii

Introduction   1

1   The room   3

2   The programme   6

3   Essential play material   9

4   More play material   20

5   Outdoor play   38

6   The interest corner   42

7   Books   51

8   Language and storytelling   56

9   Music and movement   68

10   Health and hygiene   76

11   The child in the group   85

12   Meeting intellectual needs   97

13   Spiritual growth   100

14   Language with the less voluble   103

15   The teacher's role   111

16   Supervision   116

17   Working with other adults   119

18   Parents' problems   126

19   Keeping your head above water   135

Appendix   144

A short bibliography   146

Index   147

Preface

For more than thirty years I have been a nursery school teacher, and so this book is written from that point of view, but the advice and information it contains will, I hope, be useful to many different groups of people working with pre-school children. These include nursery nurses and nursery students working in day and residential nurseries and in the children's wards of hospitals, playgroup leaders, playleaders in Playparks and One o'Clock Clubs, the staff of children's homes catering for under-fives, and a very large group—the mothers of pre-school children. In addition, I hope it will prove useful not only to young nursery school teachers, but also to reception class teachers, and to students in Colleges of Education whose training course includes work with the under-sixes.

Although the conditions under which these various groups work are so different that their approach must of necessity be different, I believe that the aim of all the work they do is the same: to help the young child to attain optimum development—emotional, social, intellectual, physical. The degree of development will vary very widely, being influenced both by inborn ability, and by the conditions in which the pre-school period is passed, but within these limits we can do a great deal to promote maximum individual growth. The importance of the relationship between the child and the adult, and between the child and other children cannot be over-emphasised, and although intensive compensatory teaching may be required for severely handicapped children, e.g. the deaf child, the 'brain-damaged', the autistic, in most cases this is given against a background of normal education with its opportunities for creative work, for exploring the environment, for learning to live in a community. All through the book I emphasise human relationships because only as persons in a community where these relationships are good can children grow towards maturity.

As head of a local authority nursery school I have a large measure of autonomy, and a generous capitation allowance, both of which make my work easier. In this book you may find activities suggested which are not possible in your particular set-up, be it home, play-group or whatever, and so I hope you will use those suggestions that are practicable, perhaps adapt others to your circumstances, and not feel guilty about disregarding those which are not applicable. By using your imagination you can make the most of even very limited circumstances, so do not underestimate the value of the work you can do. Above all—conversation is both free and priceless, and makes the most ordinary activity into an 'educational experience'.

My continual emphasis on the importance of good adult/child relationships arises from my conviction that it is in this context that the best work and the best teaching are done. As a nursery school teacher you must not stand apart: you not only prepare a rich environment, but you work in it with your children. This is very tiring, even for an experienced teacher; in the last chapter there are suggestions of ways to lighten the load.

Do not feel over-anxious about visits from inspectors and supervisors: their aim is to criticise constructively and to give help. If your group is good enough for the children in it, then it is good enough for anyone who may visit it, but if you feel it is not good enough, then ask for help and advice. Your head teacher has a great deal of practical experience and will gladly advise you if you ask her. Even if you feel that her aims and methods are perhaps somewhat out-of-date, remember that she *is* the Head, so do not make sweeping changes without discussing them with her; she will not take kindly to an assumption that because you have just finished your training, you therefore know all the answers.

From young teachers struggling to deal with situations that arise in nursery school, from students struggling with teaching practice, and from parents struggling with behaviour problems, there frequently comes the question, 'But what do you do?' I offer this book as an answer. Having worked with pre-school children for almost the whole of my career, all the suggestions come from my attempts to deal with actual occurrences—there is nothing theoretical or academic about the advice given. I have avoided impersonal forms such as 'One should . . . ' or 'It should be done . . .', and have used instead the direct 'You should . . .', whilst not meaning to imply that mine is the only right way to deal with a situation, still less that my words should be learned by rote and used as a magic formula! Throughout the book I have referred to the individual child as 'he'; this is purely a matter of convenience with no other significance; this applies also to the use of 'she' for the head teacher and school doctor. In the same way I have used 'You, the teacher' as a convenient form of address; readers from other professions are, of course, included, for most of the material is also applicable to their work.

Finally, my thanks are due to all who have helped me with this book: to my colleagues whose encouragement has cheered me and whose constructive criticisms of the manuscript have helped the book to its final shape; to Fred Pryor, of Michael Dyer Associates, whose professional prints from my amateur 'snaps' have greatly improved the quality of the illustrations; and especially to Inez Pryor, who has been my deputy for the past five years, and whose work with the children has provided me with many of my best examples. I have learned so much at my school and have received so much help and encouragement there, that I would like to express my gratitude by dedicating *Playing, Learning and Living* to all the children, parents and staff who, through the years, have been part of the Robert Owen Nursery School.

Vera A. Roberts

Introduction

About the age of three, most children are ready for a wider environment, a broader social life, and more intellectually stimulating experiences. This is the age when, having come to know himself as a person, the child begins to know others in their own right and not just as extensions of himself; when his ability to memorise and to learn is at a peak, and when he is ready to reach out to anything, from circuses to circulation of the blood, from dressing-up to drains, that catches his interest and engages his whole concentration. His growing independence urges him to go forward to explore a wider world and enables him to form relationships with children and adults outside his family circle. In short, he is ready for nursery school, which is not a substitute for his home, but rather an extension of it. It is a small community where he will make new friends, where he will be introduced to an environment which, while sufficiently the same each day to give him security, is sufficiently different to be stimulating, in which he will be encouraged to observe, to experiment, to make messes and to make mistakes, and where he will be helped to consolidate the knowledge and experience he has gained, both by being given the opportunity to repeat it and by talking about it with his teacher.

What benefits does he gain from this experience? I put emotional security in a wider circle first, because this is essential for full development. This security is not a shelter from unhappiness and tribulation, but is rather the ability to deal with these, which comes from the child's knowledge that he is accepted for what he is: he can mature emotionally because he is neither treated like a baby nor exhorted to 'be a man'. His social development is promoted by his play with other young children: he is free to be friends and to quarrel, to lead and to follow, to be father (and mother!) and baby, a policeman and a prisoner. Through role-playing he learns who he is, who others are, and what it feels like to be them. Intellectual growth is encouraged by the stimulating environment in which he is led to observe, to experiment, to question, to discuss. He learns how to learn, rather than accumulating a number of facts. Through free experimentation with materials he builds up a body of experience from which to form adequate concepts; by talking and listening he develops his language ability.

And yet these benefits are available to only a very small proportion of our pre-school children. With the present shortage of places in nursery schools, children too often can be admitted only if they suffer from some social or emotional handicap such as a broken home or a behaviour problem, whilst those with a physical or mental handicap seldom find a place however great their need. In some areas, the normal child from a stable home has no hope at all of nursery education.

Educational thought is becoming increasingly aware of the importance of the pre-school years, and of the great disadvantages imposed on many children who have not attended nursery school before starting compulsory schooling at the age of five. Because of this, and also because of pressure from parents and educators, the Government is showing somewhat more interest in pre-school children, and through the Urban Aid programme has allowed increased expenditure on this age group in the Educational Priority Areas in 1969/70; but as modern research stresses ever more strongly the need to develop fully the child's abilities at this stage, it is vital that successive governments expand the pre-school provision until a nursery school place is available for every child. It rests on those of us who are nursery teachers not only to teach the children for whom we are responsible, but to show the educational value of the child-centred approach.

And now to work!

1

The Room

Most of us are faced with a rectangular room into which to fit the activities and equipment we provide. You can make this shape more interesting, creating corners and bays, by putting cupboards at right angles to the walls instead of flat against them, and by using clothes-horse screens to divide the remaining area. Be careful to leave sufficient open space for the free circulation of children, adults, dolls' prams and lorries. The room must be arranged before the children arrive so that it looks gay, welcoming, stimulating, and you are free to greet the children and their parents. (This does not mean that the children should not help with mixing dough, collecting cookery equipment, preparing paint and so on, but these jobs must be done in such a way that the children are involved in the work and are not just looking on, or waiting around for the material to be ready for their use.)

I will not try to suggest an ideal room arrangement, because this depends on its size and shape, the position of doors and windows, the presence or lack of a sink, but there are a few points to be borne in mind. The brick play should be in an area large enough for really big constructions but not on a 'through route', the home corner should be big enough for several children to play together, the book corner should be in a good light, as should the interest corner, the water play should be near the sink or near the door to the water supply, but also in a warm part of the room, the clay table should not be close enough to the sand for the two to mix, and so on.

You will find it helpful to work out a plan on paper, to try it out, and then to modify it in the light of experience. When you have a workable plan, there is still no need to keep rigidly to it. Sometimes

3

to put equipment in a different part of the room gives it a new interest, though it is not good to change it so frequently that the children never know where to find anything. Children enjoy floor play and you can arrange for this by providing mats or floor blankets. Jigsaws are better on a mat than a blanket, since the pieces may well get mislaid in the folds, while it is useless to expect successful brick-building on a blanket as every movement will topple the structure. When you have decided on suitable positions for the main equipment, arrange storage for it near at hand. Hang the paper container near the easel, keep the clay equipment in a cupboard near the clay table, put the music stand near the piano, and so on; this will save a great deal of unnecessary walking about by children and staff.

Many items of equipment need containers, which can be improvised and made to look attractive. Tins and boxes can be covered with bright paper or 'Contact', or can be painted, and should be renovated or renewed as often as necessary. Plastic washing-up bowls and food containers can often be bought cheaply at sale time; the rectangular shape usually fits better on the shelves. The children enjoy scrubbing bricks, washing dolls and dolls' clothes, polishing furniture, and can be made more aware of the need to use equipment carefully if they help to take care of it. When every item has its appointed place it is easy to check that everything is there, and the children learn to put things away when they have finished with them. You must also check that the cupboard tops are kept tidy and that the piano has nothing but music books on it.

Display is an important part of arranging the room. You will want to put up some of the children's work, but do not use it to cover every inch of the walls! You should not take a child's work for display without first asking his permission; neither should you decline to display a child's work because you feel it does not reach a desired standard: all honestly done work is valid. Paintings should be neatly mounted and the child's name and perhaps the title written clearly, so long as it does not detract from the picture. If the walls have soft-board or wooden panels for display, fix the work with dress-making pins put in at an angle of 45 degrees—these are less obtrusive than drawing pins. If you have no display panels, work can be put up by putting loops of masking tape on the back and pressing it carefully on the wall. Make sure the pictures are straight by looking at them from the other side of the room: display pictures, posters and topical illustrations in the same way.

You will want to have flowers and foliage in your room. Provide some suitable vases—*not* jam-jars—and make sure each morning that they are filled with water and any dead flowers removed. The children may bring flowers to school, anything from a couple of dandelion heads to a bunch from the florist, and these must be welcomed and the bringer helped to put them in water.

One last point: when your room is as attractive as you can make it, *kneel down* and look at it. You will then have some idea of how it appears to the children: you may find that the pictures are too high to be seen clearly and that the flowers on the cupboard are out of sight, whereas the paint on the table-legs is only too visible! Act accordingly.

2

The Programme

When you are planning the programme, put first a long period of free (undirected) activity. This should be not less than one and a quarter to one and a half hours, and is essential whether the children attend half-day or full time. The emphasis is on the provision of a rich play environment, with freedom for each child to choose his own activity and to continue with it as long as he wishes, and so, although milk can be served informally, the period should not be interrupted for organised groups such as story or music. During this time the children should be free to play indoors or out, weather permitting, and you should consider the outdoor provision as carefully as the indoor.

In the full-day school it will be necessary towards the end of the morning to clear away at least some of the play material in order to make room for the midday meal; you may find this is a good time for a story group, as long as you can be certain of an uninterrupted ten to fifteen minutes. When the story has ended, some children can go to wash their hands, some can help lay the tables, whilst the rest play until it is time for them to wash. If you have a 'buffet service' meal no child need sit around waiting for others, but if you have 'family tables', then you must ensure that there is some interesting 'clean' activity for those who have washed: this may be an informal group sitting with you on a blanket for finger-play rhymes, or it may be a peaceful time with books and table toys. When the children have finished their meal, they will need to go to the lavatory and wash their hands before the rest period, which is discussed in a later chapter. In the afternoon arrange a music time for those who want to take part, but also ensure that there is a good variety of play material again available for the children's use, or they will waste time in a desultory way until taken home. The afternoon play may well be less vigorous, less intense than in the morning, but should still be varied and purposeful. There must never be a time when everything has been cleared away and the children sit wearing their outdoor clothes, waiting to be called for. Those who leave first should just put away their own equipment; the last few to leave may help with some clearing up, being encouraged to 'make the room ready for tomorrow'. After they have all gone home, finish the tidying, make sure any livestock has been attended to, and leave the room ready for the cleaner.

In the half-day school the pace is somewhat quicker, and you have to fit everything necessary into two and a half to three hours. There are several ways of doing this: after many experiments, I have found the following arrangements very satisfactory. The children arrive between 9.10 and 9.30 and work with their chosen play material until about 11 o'clock. They usually change their activities several times, and are invited to have their milk, biscuit and apple during one such break. Shortly before 11 o'clock, we clear away the messy activities—paint, clay, water, etc., and put out chairs and/or a blanket for story-time. I encourage all the children to come for a story, as it is our only 'together time' in the session, but do not insist on this. After the story we have ten to fifteen minutes music, ending about 11.45, when the children begin to go home; they have usually all gone by 12 noon. If we are not having a set music time, the story begins later, about 11.25, and is followed by finger-play rhymes, songs, and conversation about anything of general interest. Those who are not called for at 11.45 have the opportunity to play quietly in the room or to help tidy up 'ready for the afternoon children'. The afternoon session, from 1.30 to 4 p.m. is slightly shorter, but is arranged in a similar way.

This programme is offered as a guide, and not as a pattern that must be copied exactly. If you have two rooms available, as in some nursery classes, you can clear one for story and music, leaving the other available for play. You may prefer to have music first, followed by a story, though this has the disadvantage that, if the children have danced with bare feet, the quicker will have to sit waiting, while the slower struggle with their shoes and socks. However you vary the programme, *always* keep the long play period at the beginning of the session, so that children can get to work as soon as they arrive. When you have planned it, look at it carefully to make sure that you are not wasting the children's time at any point in the day, and then try it out over a period of time, but do not be slavishly bound by it: an unexpected visitor, the first spring day, sudden involvement in some new interest, are all reasons for forgetting the timetable and enjoying the present.

3

Essential Play Material

There are certain play materials which you must provide, however limited the space and however difficult the circumstances. These materials need not be expensive and the arrangements need not be elaborate. You will, as and when possible, want to supplement them with additional material, which will be discussed in a later section. Remember that children need to play in and out of doors whenever possible.

Sand

For indoor use, this should be silver sand, which is fine and non-staining. Most educational suppliers sell special sand trolleys, which should be low enough for the smaller children to reach, heavy enough to prevent the trolley 'walking' in use, but light enough to move for cleaning, etc. Castors at one end help mobility, whilst sturdy legs at the other help to anchor it in one position. The base of the inner sand container should be strong enough to stand up to vigorous play: old-fashioned galvanised may well be more satisfactory than modern plastic. Wood is not advisable—the damp sand will rot it. If money is scarce, you may be able to buy a bungalow bath cheaply at a sale, or even obtain an outsize enamel bowl. Either of these may be stood on low boxes or on the floor, but not on a table, or it will be too high for the children to reach. If you have space it is good to provide both damp sand and dry sand, but if not, the damp sand can sometimes be allowed to dry out. It can also sometimes be made very wet—what the children call sloppy sand, or coffee ice-cream. Buckets and spades are necessary; these may be made of wood or plastic, but not metal—not only does it rust, but a quick-tempered child can inflict a nasty wound with a tin spade. Provide also variously-shaped moulds, spoons and scoops, sieves and funnels for the dry sand, and a length of plastic or rubber tubing. Small cars are useful for sand-box layouts, and also some toy people. Keep a dustpan and brush handy to deal with spills. Children can be expected to play carefully, but it is inevitable that some sand gets on the floor, and it will quickly tread all over the room unless dealt with. This not only wastes the sand, and makes the room untidy, but also antagonises the cleaner! The sand that is swept up may need to be washed and drained before being used again, and must be dried as well before being put back into the dry sand bin. At night the cover should be left off the damp sand, in order to keep it fresh, and the sand toys taken out to dry off.

It is important to make a firm rule that no child is to throw sand: explain that it may damage another child's eyes. This rule *must* be kept. Sand should be immediately washed out of eyes, and, if pain persists, the child should see a doctor, in case the eyeball has been scratched. A child with eczema should have medical approval for sand play: it may be possible to provide cotton gloves with close-fitting wrists to protect the skin.

When you are playing with the children at the sand, talk about the feel of it, the dampness and dryness, the patterns you can make in damp sand, the way dry sand runs like water, but doesn't make you wet. Dry sand is heavier than damp—why? What happens when damp sand becomes dry?

If an outdoor sandpit can be provided it should have a wire-netting or other ventilated cover to keep out the cats, and it must have adequate drainage. If it has not been used for some time, take off the top layer of dirty sand and, if necessary, wash it through with a hose, before allowing the children to use it. Much more adventurous work can be undertaken in the outdoor sand. A group of children can dig out a river bed, or a castle with a moat round it, and carry out buckets of water to fill the river or the moat. Be careful this play does not get out of control, so that the children get wet feet and muddy clothes. If a child has, for health reasons, to be excluded from sand play, let him help you with the hose or in bringing buckets of water, or ensure that there is something exciting that he can do instead.

Water

As for the sand, a suitable container is necessary, but can be improvised if you cannot afford a purpose-built one. Remember that it will be very heavy with water in it, and so consider how you will empty it. The sides should be at least 15 cm high, with not more than 5 cm of water, or the children will find it impossible not to slop it over. Waterproof aprons are essential: a temporary makeshift is to staple tape ties to polythene sheeting, but this is not durable, and has the great disadvantage that the water runs off and wets the child's feet. It is, therefore, worthwhile making satisfactory aprons as described on page 144. You must provide funnels, tubing, receptacles for filling and pouring, things that float and things that sink, etc. Avoid glass articles as too fragile, and dangerous when broken. A washing-up liquid container makes a good fountain; others with nail-holes in the sides allow water to spout out at different levels. A plastic tank, holding about 5 litres, and with a handle at the top and a tap at the bottom, may be stood on a shelf across the water tray. This shelf should be slightly longer than the width of the tray, and should have blocks fastened underneath to prevent it slipping in. In cold weather the water should be warm, and should be topped up with warm water during the session, and the water-play arranged in a warm part of the room. It can be put outside in warm weather, but not when it is at all chilly. You may like sometimes to colour the water with cochineal or a blue-bag, and sometimes to add washing-up liquid, but do let them use ordinary plain water sometimes! Keep a floor-cloth handy to wipe up spills, and encourage the children to deal with their own mishaps. Water play sometimes increases a child's need to pass water: be alert to this possibility, and remind unreliable children of their need to go to the lavatory.

At the water tray, discuss what 'full' means—not nearly full—and what emptiness is. Talk about floating and sinking, absorbent like a sponge and non-absorbent like metal, rusting and non-rusting, melting and dissolving. Ben, when nearly four, made a wooden boat, and then asked me how to make an anchor. I suggested drawing one on paper and then cutting it out. He looked at me scornfully, walked off without a word, and came back with a piece of lino, asking 'Will *this* melt in water?' You can demonstrate how to fill a narrow-necked container through a funnel. You can ask why water does not come out of a hole above the water-line. You can verbalise and interpret the children's experiments, introducing them to such terms as 'half-full', 'half-empty', 'running over', etc. In the winter you can do things with snow and ice, in the summer with ice-cubes, if there is a refrigerator on the premises. Sand and water play often overlap, particularly in the play possible outside. Inside it is better to put your dry sand tray at some distance from the water tray!

Bricks

Try to provide at least three types of bricks:

a Large hollow bricks that can be built into really big structures. If you cannot afford those made of plywood and obtainable from educational suppliers, see if you can persuade a tobacconist to give you empty cigar boxes, which can be glued shut or fastened with pin-nails. Keep to two or three standard sizes or building will be frustrating.
b Small solid blocks, of beech or some other non-splintering wood. These should be of various sizes but based on a square, a good size for which is 8 × 8 × 4 cm. If these are home-produced, they *must* be cut accurately, with right-angles, or they will be useless for building.
c Strips of wood for roads, bridges and flyovers, together with squares and oblongs of plywood for roofs and floors.

BRICK STORAGE

If it can be afforded, a folding library cupboard makes excellent storage for the hollow bricks. It can be opened and used as a room divider, then closed and pushed away when the space is needed. Failing this, wooden fruit crates can be sandpapered and painted (by the children) and stood on end, side by side. Smaller bricks can be kept in a box on wheels: this must not be too deep, or small children will not be able to reach the bottom: 80 × 45 × 35 cm is a good average size. Do not have a container that requires the bricks to be fitted in exactly—this is a waste of time and patience.

Provide some cars and lorries, etc. both for transporting the bricks and for driving on the roads, and also some people to inhabit the towns, houses, etc; these latter can be very simple. Animals for farms, homes and zoos should be included—sturdy wooden shapes, rather than small metal models which may get trodden on and bent. Open toy-shelves on the walls make good storage for these items: small diagrammatic drawings may be stuck on the wall at the back to show where the various items should be put away.

If you find that the bricks are being neglected by the children, try providing something new in the corner, or perhaps setting up a simple construction before the children arrive. Show interest in their work, discussing its progress, and perhaps suggesting additions and refinements. A newspaper cutting of a new flyover, or a catalogue illustration of children playing with bricks may be put up in the brick corner, as may photographs of work done, if you are able to produce them.Whilst you are talking to the children at their work, introduce such phrases as 'taller than', 'shorter than', 'twice as long', 'too narrow', etc. Three-year-old Graham spoke of a brick as being not the right 'shortth', and refused to accept 'length' as the correct term: 'No, it's too long, not too short'. In addition to these mathematical terms, let them talk about their fantasies, which are often played out in the brick corner. You must not intrude, but by showing interest, and, perhaps, asking a simple question such as, 'Why did he do that?' or making a non-committal comment, you will give the child the opportunity to talk out something on his mind, whether it be trouble at home or a disturbing television programme. Do not attempt psychological interpretations. Do be sensitive to fantasy.

Clay

Don't be content with Plasticine: clay is a 'must'. It can be either the red or the grey variety, though I find the red easier to keep in good condition. If your tables have a Formica surface, no covering is necessary as the clay washes off very easily. Individual boards are not necessary either; they may, in fact, be a disadvantage as they tend to slip about when the children work vigorously. Provide several balls of clay (with some kept in reserve), wooden rollers—a cut-up broom handle, wooden spatulae for cutting the clay, and a variety of small objects for patterns and texturing—e.g. buttons, fir-cones, the green outer cases of sweet chestnut, and shells. A few pieces of cardboard, papier-mâché eggbox lids, supermarket polystyrene trays should be available for children who want to save their work. Vary the accessories you provide—sometimes twigs, sometimes feathers, sometimes just fingers can be used. Vary also the amount of clay provided, to encourage work on a large or a tiny scale. While the average ball of clay may be the size of a small grapefruit, sometimes you will put out tiny balls, perhaps a quarter of this size, sometimes you will supply a large quantity, perhaps covering the whole table surface. Your stock of clay should be kept in a tightly closed container, even if this is nothing more elaborate than a polythene sack. A smaller container with a well-fitting lid, such as a food-storage box, can be used for the clay in current use. At the end of the session, make the clay into cubes or balls; if it is a little dry, press your thumb in, and put a little water in the resulting depression. If you find the clay too sticky for use at the beginning of the session, try wrapping the balls in newspaper and leaving for a few minutes. Always encourage the children to help you with preparing and clearing up the clay, and explain to them why it is necessary to add water, etc. The clay tools must be wiped with a damp cloth, or washed if they are very dirty, so that they are clean and attractive. Always look on the floor under the clay table—large pieces of clay should be salvaged, smaller pieces swept up. Think of the cleaner.

The children working with clay should wear aprons and have their sleeves rolled up. You should not demonstrate how to use the material or how to make models, but it is helpful if you sit down with the children and work with your own lump of clay, thus unobtrusively demonstrating techniques, whilst not producing an example to copy. Talk about their work and yours, and encourage effort rather than give too much praise for individual achievements: the value is in the involvement in the work rather than in the finished product. You will find that they become totally involved in work with clay: the younger will pound and cut it, pile it up and smear it on the table; the older ones will begin to use it more purposefully, even to model with it. Both types of activity are valid. Models can be hardened by drying *slowly* (it will crack if you dry the clay too quickly), and then painted and varnished, but you should make sure that limbs, etc., are firmly attached, by smearing clay over the joint; even so, it is wise to warn the children that their work may disintegrate as it dries. By filling a small container with clay and leaving it in the air, you can demonstrate how it shrinks as it dries. When the children have finished work at the clay table, they should wash their hands and perhaps take off their aprons before going on to another activity. I like to encourage them also to clear up their clay when they stop work, and to make an attempt to shape it into a ball, unless they have made something they want to keep 'to show Mummy'.

Painting

PAPER

Plain newsprint is a satisfactory reasonably cheap paper to use, and if there is a printing works near your school it may be willing to give you ends of rolls, particularly if you show your appreciation by sometimes sending them a painting! Sugar paper and pastel paper are both good, but more expensive, and will need the paint to be mixed a little thinner. If you are limited in the amount of money you can spend on paper, it is better to buy just newsprint rather than to provide a greater variety but a smaller quantity; incidentally, children will paint quite happily on newspapers. The paper should be cut to various shapes and sizes: do not condition your children to painting only on rectangles, but offer them triangles, circles, narrow strips, and even torn shapes; but not pinked edges, please, which will detract from the painting.

Painting may be done at an easel, on a table, or on the floor, but in the latter case, make sure it will not be walked on. If an easel is used, it should be kept clean, and with paper on it ready for use: this is probably most easily done by clipping the paper at the top with two clothes pegs, which are easier for the children to manage than bulldog clips. Keep a supply of clean paper always available within the children's reach; you may find it convenient to hang a container on the wall near the easel or table.

BRUSHES

The brushes may be of two sizes, a large for general work, with a smaller for those children who want to work on smaller paper, or to put in smaller detail. Hog hair fitches are the most suitable, camel hair type brushes being too soft: I find sizes 6 and 16 satisfactory. In addition, for working on really large sheets of paper on the floor, a one-inch brush, of the type used for decorating, is satisfying. Do not allow the brushes to remain in the paint-jars overnight: they should be washed at the end of the session, rinsed under the cold tap, and stored with the bristles up.

PAINT

The three primary colours (red, blue, yellow) together with black form the necessary minimum, but other colours, especially white, may be added when possible. If you buy the colours locally, make sure they are non-toxic. Provide the paint ready mixed to a consistency that will flow smoothly from the brush, but will not drip too readily or run down the paper. The children need the paint to be immediately available, so that they can make a 'statement' whenever they wish, without having to fuss about mixing dry powder colour or scrubbing at a block—though both these may be enjoyed if provided sometimes in addition to ordinary painting. The colours should always be fresh and clean so, to prevent too much waste, it is a good idea to put out only a small quantity of each colour, about 2 to 3 cm depth in a small jar. This can be replenished or renewed as necessary during the session, and at the end the jar can be washed out and clean paint put in ready for next time. Small glass jam-jars make good containers: they are heavy enough not to tip easily when the brushes are standing in them, and the colour can be seen easily. Yoghurt pots are not so suitable, being too light. The children should be expected to wear aprons for painting, and very messy workers should have their sleeves rolled up. Provide a damp cloth for wiping up spills, but teach the children not to try to deal with a broken jar, but rather to tell you what has happened. When you have to clear up broken jars, be very careful that you collect all the glass splinters from the floor, and that you rinse the cloth extremely carefully. Broken glass should be wrapped and put in the dustbin rather than in the wastepaper basket.

WHAT TO DO WITH THE FINISHED PAINTINGS

This can become a real problem if a great deal of work is being done. The ideal is to dry them flat, but as one cannot be put on top of another that is not completely dry, this method requires more space than is usually available. I have found an extending nappy-drying rack extremely useful, but if this is not possible, a 'clothes-line' can be used. Try to put it where you will not have to 'duck' to avoid the paintings every time you go by. The important thing is to see that the paintings do not touch each other while they are still wet, that the children see that you respect them, and that they can be easily found at home time. In my school, the children have first claim on their paintings: if I want to keep one or to put one on display, I may cajole and coax, but I accept the child's decision even if it goes against me.

The Home Corner

A Home Corner can be improvised from a clothes-horse or screen covered with hardboard or curtaining, or you can make two wooden frames not less than one metre high, and hinged together at one end. To this attach hardboard which has been painted or covered with 'Contact', and then fasten the ends to two corner walls, thus creating a rectangular home area. This should be as large as possible, bearing in mind the other demands made on your floor space, and may be carpeted with carpet samples, available free from some carpet shops, which you can join by sticking them with 'Copydex' to 5 cm wide binding. This is both cheaper and longer-lasting than iron-on binding.

There is some attractive home corner furniture on sale, at a price, at the educational suppliers, but it can be easily made from wooden fruit boxes, and, if carefully done, is more durable than most mass-produced items: we are still using the cooker and dresser which I made fifteen years ago, for about 1/6d each. Dolls' cots can be made very satisfactorily from wooden tomato crates, or even from plastic stacking vegetable racks, obtainable very cheaply from Woolworths. Mattresses and pillows can be cut from thick polystyrene foam and have cotton covers detachable for washing: blankets can be knitted or crocheted from odd balls of wool. A secondhand furniture or junk shop will probably have a suitable small table which can be painted and, if necessary, have the top covered with hardboard or an offcut of Formica. It is quite easy to make chairs or stools from well-sandpapered fruit boxes, while a sink can be a box on legs, with an old tap attached to the splashback to add realism. This comprises the essential furniture: you can add a dolls' clothes cupboard or chest-of-drawers, dressing-table, ironing-board, etc. when you have time and money to spare.

A tablecloth and teaset must be provided—polythene lasts longer than rigid plastic—and some cooking utensils: the smallest size 'real' saucepan, frying-pan, kettle is better than a toy cooking-set, the pieces of which are usually too small for reasonable use. A small enamel or polythene basin and a wooden spoon help make-believe cookery, and plastic cutlery is necessary to eat the result: picnic sets are cheap and usually satisfactory, but be sure the forks do not have sharp points. 'Pretend' food can be modelled from dough and baked very slowly to harden it. Several dolls are needed; these should be of various sizes, and washable. Make simple loose-fitting clothes that can be easily taken off *and* put on again by the children; I like to have more than one set to fit each doll so that they can be kept clean and attractive. The children will enjoy washing both dolls and garments —knitted clothes made from man-made fibres rather than from wool are safer in the hands of inexperienced washerwomen; in these days of launderettes and home washing-machines you may find that they have no idea of how to wash and wring clothes. Try to obtain one or two dolls' prams: an advertisement on a local shop's board, or on the school notice board may prompt a grown-up family to offer you one as a gift, or at a very low price. An overhaul of wheels and chassis, together with a coat of paint and some bright cotton covers, will make it as attractive as a new one.

Dressing-up clothes may be hung in the home corner, or on a suitable stand kept near at hand. Long skirts, jewellery, ladies' hats, handbags and shopping baskets all help rôle-playing; a baby's feeding bottle and shawl will be welcomed by would-be mothers and would-be babies alike. Do not forget a trilby hat, a uniform cap, and other male headgear for fathers. A mirror should be provided if a dressing-table is not available.

You can expect the children to maintain a reasonable standard of tidiness in the home corner: play is not helped by having things strewn all over the floor. They may need to be taught how to do this if they are not taught to keep their things tidy at home. At the end of the play period the house should be tidied by the present occupants; this is when you can expect everything to be put in its right place.

4

More Play Material

Using Varied Materials

Children should be given open-ended creative experiences: that is to say, they should have the opportunity to use materials in new ways, to experiment, to explore possibilities, to take pleasure in the doing rather than in the end-product. There is available a number of books produced for those teachers who do not feel able to let the children's natural creative abilities have free rein in the classroom, which, together with some television programmes, show how to make a variety of objects from waste material. These have a limited value in encouraging children to see possibilities in household 'rubbish', but there is no place in the nursery school for a detailed demonstration of, for example, how to make a piggy-bank from an empty squeezy bottle. There is, of course, a place for teaching techniques, whether it be wiping the brush on the side of the paint-jar to prevent unwanted drips on the painting, or allowing the Copydex adhesive to dry a little before joining the two parts. It is allowable to show children that Indian feathers painted on stiff paper will stand up, instead of flopping in a very un-brave way when painted on kitchen paper, as it is to show them how to fix the feathers securely with paper-clips rather than with paste.

Because we want children to experiment and to try out unusual combinations it is desirable that a wide variety of materials is available in juxtaposition. I have found that three or four tables pushed together form a suitable working surface, and give space for various items to be put in the middle. If the painting easel is put next to the creative table, further experiment is encouraged, such as combining collage materials with painting. You can classify the materials we provide as two- or three-dimensional: the two-dimensional can include, in addition to paints, thick wax crayons, coloured chalks and pastels, felt-tip pens and charcoal, but not ball-point pens or thin lead pencils which make too fine a line for work which we want to be strong and bold.

The three-dimensional materials include a wide variety of waste 'junk': cartons, reels, string, tubes, scraps of material, coloured paper and foil, etc., etc., together with scissors and paste. As Matthew's mother said: 'Since Matthew has been at nursery school, we never throw anything away. Either Queenie (the Dalmatian) eats it, or we put it on the compost heap, or Matthew takes it to school.' Lavina asked one day, 'Why can't we have some of them strands?'—that is, some loosely woven material for unravelling. Four-year-old Joanne stormed because I couldn't immediately produce a spring for her to use in making Zebedee of the 'Magic Roundabout':—'This is a rotten school: they haven't even got a spring!'

Satisfactory adhesives must always be available: cellulose paste such as Polycell is a very good general purpose adhesive, and has the advantage that a large jarful can be prepared in advance, and then a small quantity put out into individual paste pots. Copydex (Edward always appropriately called it 'Stickydex') is a stronger adhesive, but needs to be used under supervision, as it is relatively expensive, and requires a special solvent to remove any spilled on clothing. Cow gum is good, and fairly cheap, but it is a little difficult for small children to manage, and also has a rather unpleasant smell. Sellotape is essential, as are push-through-and-open paper fasteners and binders, whilst a long-armed stapler, though possibly too stiff for the children to use, may enable *you* to solve some knotty problem of construction. A staple gun is useful, too, but should not be left within reach of the children, as it can be dangerous. String, wool, and elastic bands should also be available for the children.

Whilst you want to provide a good variety of materials for the creative table, it is important to see that they are presented in such a way that there is still room for the children to work. I have found that oblong foil baking cases are useful for small quantities of coloured paper, material, etc., with a larger supply readily available.

These can be put in the centre of the table, or accommodated in one or two stacking wire trays, though be careful that your 'beanstalk' does not grow so high that the smaller children cannot reach the top. Larger items, such as cartons, are better off the table, being kept in readiness at the side, perhaps in a portable cupboard made from two wooden boxes, with a curtain to cover the front when not in use. Scissors should have their own container on the table; paper fasteners, etc., can be put out in a small tin, paste can be in meat paste jars, each with its own brush, and with a damp sponge at hand for sticky fingers. A wastepaper container needs to be handy. You should also see that aprons are used by very messy workers. I reproved Abigail, a cheerful four-year-old, for covering herself with paint, but she smiled happily and said: 'But, you see, it was such a lovely picture!'

While the children are working at the creative table, try to arrange for you or your assistant to be at hand both to show interest and to encourage conversation about a child's work, and also to be aware of when adult help may prevent a child losing heart, and when a word of praise and encouragement will help him to finish the job on his own. Explain to your assistant that you do not want her to tell the children what to make, nor tell them exactly how to make something, but that she should be ready to help them to overcome any difficulties they encounter and to talk to them about what they are doing. Abigail's youngest brother, Edward (not the Stickydex Edward) used to bring to school occasionally a large paper carrier full of waste materials. He would spend the first fifteen to twenty minutes of the session sticking them together to form a precarious construction, to which he gave no name, but which he would put carefully aside to dry. At the end of the session, to his mother's despair, he took it all home again. Charles, on the other hand, used to come into school, find the encyclopaedia, turn over the pages until he found what he wanted, corner the nursery assistant, and announce, 'We are going to make *this* today'. 'This' might be a four-masted sailing vessel, a prehistoric animal, or a medieval castle. Children of this age seldom co-operate in making a group model, though sometimes a natural

'life with other children' *page 85*

leader emerges, as, for example, Ben, who was passionately interested in Indians. When I provided a set of model Indians, horses, and tepees, he organised several boys to make an Indian 'scene'. '*You* can make the trees, and *you* can make the mountains, and *you* can paint some paper blue, because we need a river, and I'll make the canoe'.

When a child has finished his construction, help him to put it 'somewhere safe', so that it can dry ready for him to take home. At the end of the session, ask him if he wants to take it, and see that it is ready for him when his mother comes. You can include her in the activity by passing some favourable comment on the finished article, or on the amount of work her child has put into it. If she is obviously too burdened with a large shopping-bag to be able to take his work as well, offer to take care of it 'until tomorrow'.

I have been dealing mainly with the three-dimensional creative work, and now want to return to the two-dimensional. When the children are working at their drawing and painting, be alert to see that they have what they need and are able to handle their materials. They may need to be shown that a large paintbrush is better for covering a large area with colour, whilst a felt-tip pen is better for a small drawing. Paintbrushes must always be returned to the right paint-jars; pens must have their tops put back after use; crayons should be in flat open boxes, so that they can be picked up easily and returned without fuss. Never ask a child 'What are you drawing?' but rather show your interest by admiring the work and perhaps asking 'Would you like to tell me about it?', though you must beware of showing so much admiration that the child feels obliged to continue painting such masterpieces, and so becomes stuck in that particular rut. You must develop an awareness, a sensitivity, to a child's feeling about his picture. If he feels you are too 'nosey', too interfering, or even just too interested, he may go away and leave it unfinished, or perhaps scribble it over with black paint. Some children lose themselves in their painting, pouring out wordless tensions and emotions, and it is no-one's business, however well-intentioned, to intrude.

'a restfulness, a completeness' *page* 32

Be careful not to be inveigled into drawing for the children: this is never advisable. ALL children can draw: that the drawing should resemble something is a convention imposed by adults or older children. Sometimes a child says 'I can't draw a bird . . . (or a horse or a lorry or whatever) Will you draw me one?' An outright refusal is not helpful, but you can explain that if *you* draw a bird, it is *your* bird and not his. On the other hand, if he thinks about a bird flying across the sky 'like this' (using hand and arm movements to represent flight), or hopping on the ground to pick up crumbs, or living in a cage at the Zoo with lots of other birds with beautiful coloured feathers, then he can make a beautiful painting all about birds. Help him to understand that there is no one right way to draw a bird—and no wrong way, either, unless he has copied or traced another's drawing. It may help him to look at some books with birds pictured in different ways; i.e. the exact pictures in the reference book for bird identification, the soaring golden yellow in Charles Keeping's 'Charlie, Charlotte and the Golden Canary', the many-coloured fantasies of the Brian Wildsmith 'Birds'.

When children have finished their paintings they should be encouraged to take them from the easel or table—or floor—and hang them to dry. For some, the making of a painting is the important part, and they have no feeling of attachment to the completed picture. Other children are anxious to have their paintings to take home, so their names should be put on them to avoid confusion.

Finger-Painting

This is an inaccurately named activity that is very popular, but which requires careful organisation if children and furniture are not to be covered with coloured paste! Do not attempt it if you are short-staffed or are likely to be interrupted frequently by visitors or demanding children. Finger-painting is most satisfying when done on a large smooth surface such as a Formica-topped table. Paper-hangers' cold water paste has a more satisfactory texture than cellulose paste, but as it goes bad rather quickly, it should be mixed fresh for each session. If you put cold or tepid water into the bowl, and then add the paste powder gradually, mixing it well with a wooden spoon, you should get a fine smooth paste without lumps. If you try to mix more paste in a bowl that already contains some, you will almost certainly make it lumpy. Do not add colouring at this stage. Children who want to finger-paint must wear adequate aprons, and have their sleeves rolled up securely well above their elbows. They must also understand that the paste must be kept on the table and not wiped on the next child's clothes or down the table legs in an absent-minded moment. Have ready a deep bowl of warm water for washing hands and arms, and also several sponges. It is better not to send children to wash their hands in the bathroom when they have been finger-painting, as they may unintentionally wreak havoc on the way! When a child wants to finger-paint, and you have tied his apron firmly and rolled up his sleeves securely, give him a spoonful of paste on the table, sufficient for him to rub over the area at his disposal, and encourage him to do this with free expansive arm movements; this may be easier for him if he is standing rather than sitting. When he has spread his paste, he can choose the colour or colours that he wants to use. You will learn by experience how much powder-colour to put on: too much clots into hard lumps and is apt to get on the floor; too little gives a wishy-washy effect. I find it helpful to keep the finger-painting colours in polythene kitchen containers with a pouring hole at the top which can be closed with a slide. If you can obtain small containers of this type that the children can handle, this is ideal, but they will need guidance in their use. In addition, I sometimes give them individual dishes of powder colour, so that they can make colour experiments by dipping their fingers in the paint and rubbing it into the paste. Finger-painting is an engrossing and soothing occupation, and I have known children who have concentrated on it for well over an hour, so it is important not to hurry them 'so that someone else can have a turn'. You must keep an eye on the consistency of the paint/paste mixture with which a child is working: sometimes a sprinkle of clean water will soften the surface for him, sometimes more paste must be added, sometimes he must be helped to wash it off and begin again.

When the child has finished, there may be a rich muddy mess on the table, or there may be a finished drawing, perhaps with patches of contrasting colour, or with a swirling pattern covering the whole surface. What do we do now? For the child, the activity itself has been the important thing, and he may have no special feeling for the end-product, unless particularly encouraged to do so by an adult. All the same, as adults, we may regret destroying a lovely piece of work, and it is often possible to take a print by carefully spreading a piece of paper over it and gently rubbing until the image is transferred. This is not encouraged by some authorities on Children's Art, because it is felt that print-making is not a sufficiently immediate experience to be suitable for this age group, but I believe its occasional use would not be too severely condemned. The child's permission should be asked before taking a print of his work.

When the child has finished, he should be helped to wash his table clean. Some quite young children are amazingly efficient at this, and will persevere until every scrap of pasty paint has been rubbed away, and the surface left clean and dry. It is fun to notice the swirling patterns made by the damp sponge in the cleaning-up process, but care must be taken that the sponge is only damp and is not lifted dripping from the bowl and splashed on to the table. When his table is clean, encourage the child to squeeze out his sponge and to clean his apron (without letting streams of water run down his legs) though he will probably need help with this. When the child has cleaned his table and his apron, he must also wash his hands and arms clean, and should be inspected—especially those areas behind the elbow that are so difficult to see—before he is sent to dry himself and to pull down his sleeves.

Finger-painting can, of course, be done on paper which should be anchored to the table by wiping underneath with a damp cloth, or on sheets of cardboard, but these are not, on the whole, as satisfactory as doing it directly on the table, because prolonged work wears away the surface of the paper or card, whilst the edges act as a frame, producing small, rather tight work, instead of the gloriously free work that is seen when a whole table top is used.

Before the children wash at the end of their work, they enjoy making handprints on a sheet of paper. This may be done with abandon all over a page, which then has the child's name put on it, or may be done once with some care on a sheet large enough for several children. When dry this can be put on the wall at a height where the children can easily reach it, so that they can cover the prints with their hands, finding out which are larger, which smaller, and which '*must* be mine, because it's just the same size!'

Printing

A formal exercise in organised printing is not suitable for pre-school children, but the exciting experience of putting paint on an object and then pressing it on paper to see what shape it makes is certainly allowable. Colour pads can be made from rounds of thick foam, cut to fit suitable containers and heavily impregnated with paint, while various kinds of paper may be provided, the best having a matt surface and a slightly absorbent quality. The children will find many objects that they want to try out; you might also provide a selection on a tray, including such things as corks, cotton-reels, leaves, feathers, string, carrots, and the outer cases of sweet chestnuts. Do not provide ready-cut potatoes to print from—this is too mechanical an activity —though, under supervision, older children can try making their own potato blocks with lino-cutting tools. Children can also make impressions on a clay slab, perhaps coat it with paint, and gently rub a sheet of paper laid on top. Do not labour printing, but let it sometimes be available for those children who like experimenting. Later you can discuss the prints with a few children; 'That's an interesting shape—I wonder what made it. What do you think?' Together with printing we might include rubbings. Making rubbings of coins—that remembered activity of so many of our childhoods—is difficult for young children as they cannot hold the object still enough to get a clear image but it is exciting to take paper and a wax crayon into the garden and rub the grain on the wooden boxes, the brick on the edge of the sand-pit, the rust-pitted surface of the swing stand. This again should not be laboured, but it can bring a new dimension of 'seeing' to an intelligent rising-five-year-old, and is an extension of the awareness of the feel of different textures that you provide by ensuring that many different materials are used in the making of the apparatus provided, e.g. a velvet dolls' coat, a silk dress, a tweed skirt for dressing-up, a wooden dolls' cot, metal wheels with rubber tyres, sandpaper at the woodwork bench.

Sewing

This is popular with boys as well as girls, and some under-fives who have been allowed to sew at home are remarkably skilful at it. At the beginning the act of sewing is sufficient—the child wants to sew, not to make something with sewing. When Cathy started at nursery school, she sat at the sewing table, chose a long narrow piece of material, stitched furiously for about two minutes, by which time she had a gathered-up ball of crumpled material dangling at the end of her thread. She jumped from her chair, and danced round the room, waving her work and chanting, 'I've done it! I've done it! My beautiful sewing—I've done it! I've done it!'

The young child who simply wants to sew will manage better with scraps of rug canvas and a large bodkin threaded with double knitting wool, the two ends joined with a knot—so that you do not have to rethread it for him after every stitch. He will also enjoy a box of large buttons, which can be sewn on with large oversewing stitches.

For rather more advanced children, provide a wider selection of materials. Loosely woven cotton or wool fabric is easier to manage than rayon or silk. Felt is easy to sew, though expensive to provide. Oddments of lace and frilling appeal to dressy little girls, whilst strips of material are useful for apron strings and shoulder bag straps. I find that the most satisfactory sewing thread for nursery school children is Clark's Coton-à-Broder, used double in a size 5 crewel needle. It is rather expensive, though possibly cheaper if bought through an educational supplier, but if the hank is cut in half and loosely knotted, or, better still, is wound on to a strip of card before use, there will be no waste, and an initial outlay on six different colours will probably be enough for the whole term. Scissors sharp enough to cut material must, of course, be provided, and the children (and sometimes the staff also) must be taught to cut on the table and not on their laps, or you may have to apologise to mothers for cut clothing.

The children will decide what they want to make, but will probably need your help in cutting it out and pinning it together. Some are content with simple objects like a shoulder-bag or an apron, but many will want to make dolls' clothes, usually for an absent doll, about whose exact size they are extremely vague, expecting you to identify her by her name—'You know, it's France' (all Rachel's dolls seemed to be called France); or by her activity—'You know, the one that sits on my little swing'. (Clare, aged four). Matthew set about making a sweater for his duck, and, being a perfectionist, insisted that it must fit, which was hard on both of us, whereas Sarah managed a shift dress, complete with black lace trimming round the neck, armholes, and bottom, without strain for either herself or her teacher. Once the article is ready for stitching, it is helpful to start it off with a stitch or two but leaving the child to decide whether he will do running stitch or over-sewing, or, more probably, a mixture of the two. Do not try to teach them to hem, or to take tiny stitches, but do keep an eye to see that he is sewing in the right direction, for it is upsetting for him to discover that he has worked extremely hard at sewing up the bottom of a dress when he thought he was doing the side seam. Make sure the work is 'finished off' either by you or by him, before the thread is cut. Although you do not expect small even stitches, you can point out to him that money will fall out from the shoulder-bag whose sides are held together with only two large stitches, whilst the finished garment will be too small for the doll if the stitches are taken too far in. A certain amount of help is justifiable, but *I* refuse to put the needle in for *every* stitch if the child's only contribution is to pull it through!

As sewing requires a good deal of adult help it should be undertaken only when there is adequate staffing, and you must make certain that you are able to give your attention to the other activities also. On the other hand, experimental sewing materials can be available even when you are not free to help.

Woodwork

Your greatest problem here will probably be the supply of suitable wood. You can appeal to the parents for help: over the years I have received broken-up boxes from the greengrocer, large triangles of blockboard left over from a flooring scheme, a bag full of chunky pieces from a timber yard, and a cardboard shoebox full of coffin offcuts! These last, being hardwood, could not be used at the bench, but were a welcome addition to the brick corner. You may find a local woodworking factory willing to give you offcuts, a timber yard that will sell or even give you sacks of oddments, or a Do-It-Yourself shop that will keep your sack in a corner and fill it with oddments too small for sale. You can also approach the woodwork master if there is a boys' secondary school near at hand.

A small-size bench with a vice is useful, though not essential, but if an old table is used, provide G-cramps for holding the wood while the children saw it. Tools must be real tools, though smaller than full size—toy tools are useless. Supply several hammers, a pair of pincers, one or two saws—coping saws are generally more satisfactory than tenon saws, as the blades can be replaced cheaply, instead of having to be re-sharpened. Ovals are better nails to use—they do not split the wood so easily as the round wire nails—and more than one length is needed: I suggest 20 mm, 35 mm and 50 mm. You also need a bradawl and a screw driver, with a supply of screws for any child able to use them. If possible, supply yourself with a selection of bits and a brace. You will receive a good deal of admiration: 'Coo! My dad's got one of them,' and some good advice: 'It goes through better if you lean on it,' as well as finding it useful for various making and mending jobs.

The wood for the children's use can be kept in a suitable box under the bench or table. A few nails of each size should be in flat tins on the bench, with plenty more available for the asking. Tools can be kept in racks at the end of the bench, or in tool clips attached to a piece of board. If you paint silhouettes of the tools on the board, you can see at a glance if anything is missing.

Certain safety rules *must* be observed at the woodwork bench: e.g. tools must never be used to threaten or attack anyone; hammering must be done with care for other children's hands—and do watch for the child who tries to increase his power by swinging his hammer behind his head, because he may do an injury to an innocent bystander. In addition, I find it safer to 'start' a nail for a child who is having difficulty, rather than to expose my finger and thumb to his uncertain aim.

As with sewing, some children are content just to 'do woodwork' and have no urge to produce anything. Give them one or two thick blocks into which to hammer an endless supply of nails: they should not be allowed to knock them into the bench or the garden equipment, though Michael spent nearly an hour one afternoon 'mending' one of the ammunition boxes for me. More advanced children may be encouraged to select suitable pieces of wood from that supplied, but may need help in measuring and cutting, if two pieces the same size are required. Even quite experienced children may need to be shown why it is more satisfactory to nail a thin piece of wood to a thicker piece, rather than vice-versa. They will also need to be shown how to measure the nail against the thickness of the wood, so that they do not nail their work to the bench.

Sandpaper may be provided, for although they cannot be expected to achieve a high finish, some children will be glad to rub away the rough ends resulting from inexpert sawing. Remember to point out the difference in 'feel' of sandpapered and unsandpapered wood. Finished work can be painted, the powder colour that is used for painting pictures being quite satisfactory, but make sure the child's name is still visible or there may be confusion at home time.

If your playroom walls and ceiling are so constructed that they absorb noise, you can bring the woodwork indoors in bad weather, but the bench should be stood on a thick mat or folded floor blanket. If you already have noise problems because of an old building without sound-absorbing surfaces, do not try to have the woodwork inside, but wait until the weather is suitable for working out-of-doors, or you will so raise the noise level that the children will have to shout to make themselves heard.

Table Toys

These may be divided into three groups:—

a jigsaws, grading toys, etc.
b constructional toys
c group games.

These toys can be very expensive, and you must beware of devoting too much of your budget to equipment that has comparatively little value.

a JIGSAWS should be in fitting trays, so if they are supplied loose, it is well worthwhile making some trays with hardboard and quarter round beading, both of which can be bought at a Do-It-Yourself shop. A few children are very good at jigsaws, and will spend a lot of time doing one after another. This ability does not seem to be related to intelligence; indeed, the very intelligent children do not, as a rule, spend much time on them. As mentioned elsewhere, there is a restfulness, a completeness, that is sensed by a very stormy or tired child, who 'breaks up' a puzzle, and then gradually repairs the 'damage', making the picture whole again. Try and teach the children not to leave a puzzle unfinished, but to ask for help if they are unable to do it alone.

GRADING TOYS seem to be out of fashion these days, though a few of those made by Kiddicraft are still popular, e.g. 'Billy and his seven barrels'. Nesting boxes that can be built into a tall tower are welcome, but beware of improvising with some nesting tins, for the noise is nerve-shattering when the tower inevitably tumbles.

Both grading toys and jigsaws must be complete, so check that there are no pieces missing before they are put away. Any that are not complete can be put aside for a few days, to see if the missing piece turns up. It is sometimes possible to make an acceptable replacement piece for a jigsaw if you know someone who is good with a fretsaw.

b CONSTRUCTIONAL TOYS are of two kinds:—those of the type

that can be unscrewed and screwed together again to make the same lorry, aeroplane or whatever, and those consisting of a number of standard parts which can be built into different models. The first have only a limited value—and a very limited popularity—and I would not recommend you to buy them for nursery school. The second type should be provided whenever possible, the wooden sets being better than those made of plastic. It is possible to start with a small set and to add to it year by year until you have enough for several children to work together. Some of these constructional sets come complete with diagrams for making various models, but I prefer to dispense with the diagrams and let the children work freely from their imagination.

It is not feasible to check that no pieces are missing before putting away these toys, but you can teach the children to look under as well as on the table when clearing up—and do try to show appreciation when a child brings you a piece he has found somewhere, even if it *is* in the middle of music and movement and you feel his attention should not have strayed.

c GROUP GAMES are not often used in nursery school, but I think they can sometimes be welcome, perhaps during a long spell of bad weather when the children may have become a little restless and are glad of some teacher-directed activity. Such games include Picture Lotto (known to some of them as Bingo), Snap, Picture Dominoes, The Memory Game, an easy dice game called The House that Jack Built, and a comparatively new game called Connect, which is very popular with some four-year-old boys, who respond to the challenge of fitting the small square cards correctly to make long lines of red and blue and black. It is well worthwhile covering the individual cards of these games with clear Contact before using them, for it considerably lengthens the life of the game, and makes it possible to keep them reasonably clean. Care must be taken to see that all the cards are collected at the end of the game, and the sets should be checked occasionally to make sure they are complete.

It is not always necessary to have an adult in charge of these group games: some four-year-olds can quite successfully initiate and carry through a game of Lotto or Dominoes. Snap seems to be more difficult for them, possibly because of the different rules used in different homes, whilst the Memory Game is in itself rather difficult, and so an adult is necessary to keep it going, though the cards can be used for matching when it is not in use as a group game.

Traffic Toys

Although you will have included cars, trains, boats, etc., with the blocks in the brick corner, try to find room for some smaller toys, such as the Matchbox series, that can be used on a table-top, perhaps with a miniature train set and a model town. The play value of this equipment is greatly increased if roads, and railways are painted on a board that fits the table-top; you may even be able to make this a plan of the district, showing, for example, the road that leads to the school, the local shopping centre and the railway station. If you are very short of space in the playroom, utilise the wooden top of the sand or water trolley for this play, so that when sand and water are not in use, the traffic toys may be put out.

Traffic play is a good conversation stimulus, and is also a valuable outlet for aggression, enabling multiple crashes to be arranged. The wear and tear on the vehicles is enormous, so try to keep them fresh and attractive with a new coat of paint and some new tyres. As one of my three-year-olds said recently: 'We don't like broken buses, do we?'

Dough

This can be provided once or twice a week instead of clay, but it is a less versatile material, and so is not suitable as a permanent substitute. Make your dough from plain flour, not self-raising, and mix it carefully with cold water, kneading it well so that it is not sticky in the middle. The addition of a little salt to the flour will help to keep it, while one tablespoonful of cooking oil greatly improves the texture. You can also add a little powder colour to the flour if you prefer tinted pastry. Make enough dough to provide at least four portions not smaller than a Jaffa orange, but do not make enough for a long period as it will not keep. Provide the children with rolling-pins—perhaps a sawn-up broom handle they have helped to sandpaper, biscuit cutters and small bun tins: if you have Formica-topped tables, pastry boards are unnecessary, and, indeed, are difficult for small children to manage, as they slide under pressure.

A semi-permanent modelling dough can be made by mixing two cupfuls of flour, one of salt, and a tablespoonful of alum (obtainable from a chemist) with sufficient cold water. This can be used for modelling home-corner 'food'. If set aside for a few days to harden, it can then be painted with ordinary powder paint, and will stand up to a certain amount of hard wear in use, though it will disintegrate if thrown or stamped on, as I discovered when Maria was in a temper!

Cooking

This is a time-and-attention-consuming activity that is well worth-while trying to include in your programme occasionally.

There may be certain safety regulations laid down by your Local Authority, so please check with your head teacher that these will not be infringed before you start. If it is not possible for you to have a small oven for the children to use, you can still do some 'cooking'. Peppermint creams are easy, involving only icing sugar, peppermint essence and water. The resulting mix can be rolled out, tasted, cut into shapes with tiny cutters, and set aside to dry. You will be able to find further sweet recipes that require no cooking, perhaps in a book from the Library. Another uncooked food is jelly: the struggle to pull the cubes apart, their gradual disappearance as they dissolve in the hot water, the opportunity to dip a finger in a spill occasioned by too vigorous stirring, the spooning out into small moulds, the continual running to see if it has set, all add up to an exciting experience which culminates in a jelly party in the home corner.

If you have the use of an electric boiling ring, your scope is widened. You can make custard or blancmange to pour over the jelly:

it looks unpleasant if the jelly has not set, but apparently tastes delicious! You can have a Pancake Party on Shrove Tuesday. You can cook sausages for a Guy Fawkes or a Hallowe'en Party. You can cook fresh vegetables: it is surprising how few children know that peas come out of pods as well as tins, or that sweet corn grows on the cob before it is put in a plastic bag in the deep freeze. It is not advisable to try to make sweets that involve boiling the mixture, because boiling sugar is very very hot, and can give a nasty burn if spilt or splashed on a child's hand.

Once you have an oven at your disposal your scope is limited only by the cost of the ingredients and the ease of preparation. There is no need to make rock buns every week for two years, as Sarah's mother told me her elder daughter had done at *her* nursery school. Jam tarts, bread pudding (the recipe was accurately given, in great detail, by Hayley), apple pie (Peter made one to celebrate his fifth birthday, and, unusually at a loss for words, could only say 'Ooh! Ooh!' when he saw that his rather grey pastry had turned golden-brown in the oven), or even a 'celebration cake with yellow icing on the top and purple roses, because I'm going to Canada' (four-year-old Andrew). Whatever you or the children choose, make sure that the major part of the work is able to be done by them.

When you plan a cooking session, talk it over with the children the day before. Give them an opportunity to decide what to make, and discuss what ingredients will be needed, perhaps sending two children across the road with your assistant to buy what you lack. You may also need to decide whose turn it is to cook, so that it is not always the children who arrive first who get the chance. The next day you collect together everything you will need, before the children arrive, so that no time is wasted when you are ready to begin. The children should wash their hands and put on a cookery apron before they start, and, under supervision, they can turn on the oven. Help each child to weigh out the ingredients, telling him the names of the weights and showing him how to make the scales balance. He also needs to learn how much is a pinch of salt, how much a level spoonful, how much a heaped spoonful. The child whose mother does no baking at home will need to be shown how to cream fat and sugar, how to rub fat into flour, etc., though you will find that almost everyone knows how to break an egg—but be on the look-out for children like Roy who, saying 'I know how to break an egg', picked one up and crushed it in his hand! The children can be shown how to grease the bun-tins and how to cut the pastry to fit the pie. They can, with care, put their own cooking into the oven, but only the most skilful will be able to take it out with the help of the oven cloth. When the cooking is finished, they should help with the washing-up and putting away. Four children are probably as many as you can help at one time, but there is sure to be a number of spectators. Try not to become so involved with the techniques that you are too busy to seize all the wonderful conversation opportunities. Talk not only about what you are doing, but also about Mummy's cooking at home, school cooks getting dinner ready, men and women in factories preparing tinned and packaged food. Talk also about where the ingredients come from, why we eat food and what happens to it. Talk about weighing and measuring, hot and cold, underdone and burned. And let them talk about their cooking and eating experiences.

The food cooked should be treated with respect and eaten with some ceremony. The cooks may pass round a plate of biscuits at story-time or the buns may be put in a tin and served with the next day's milk. They will probably want to take home a taster for Mummy, and you must make sure that each child takes something that *he* has made, and not just a biscuit from the common plate. I have found it very satisfactory to give the children foil dishes to cook in; it is then easy to put a slip of paper with the child's name on it on each dish as it comes out of the oven. There should be no difficulty in collecting a sufficient supply of these dishes from mothers who buy ready-to-eat foods.

When cooking, as when sewing and finger-painting, remember that although most of your attention is given to this activity, the other children are still your responsibility, and make sure your assistant is free to attend to them, being interested in what they do and say, and giving whatever help is necessary.

5

Outdoor Play

Never feel that outdoor play is unimportant, that it does not matter, that supervision from the safety angle is all that is necessary. The teacher's interest and assistance is needed just as much when the children are playing outside as it is when they are indoors, and you should never just 'turn them out' so as to have some peace! So we will consider outdoor play in five sections.

1 There is the large apparatus, often similar to but rather smaller than that provided in the parks. This large equipment is usually supplied by the local education authority, but it is your responsibility to see that it is maintained in a safe condition. Although it may be available to the children in their local park, that is no reason for its not being used at school. The 'jungle gym' serves not only as a climbing frame, but also as a house, a space rocket, a fire-engine, a pirate ship, or a beleaguered fort from which to fight off one's enemies. The swing offers not only vigorous exercise, but a refuge in sadness and a soothing rhythm for fretted nerves. The slide, the nesting-bridges and planks, and the rest of the large apparatus are all used for imaginative play as well as for physical activity. There must, of course, be supervision so that the children play reasonably safely—though it is impossible to exclude every potentially dangerous activity—and certain rules must be laid down, and kept, e.g. that you only come down the slide from the top and do not climb up from the bottom, that you never run in front of the swing, that you do not hoist dangerously heavy objects on to the climbing frame but, just as

'sturdy wooden shapes are needed in the brick corner'
page 13

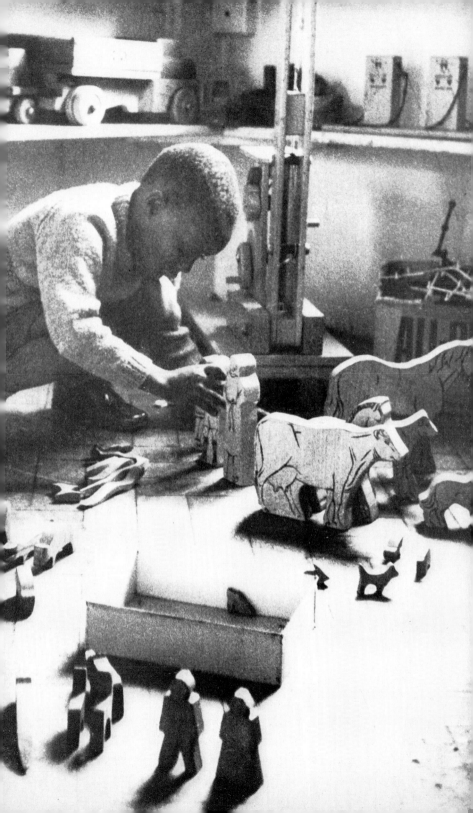

important, there must be interest and encouragement: 'If you stretch just a *little* bit more, you will be able to reach the bar'; 'You're not frightened of the slide any more, are you?' Remember also the value to less privileged children of learning the meaning of prepositions in their own bodies: 'Now you are UP', 'Now you slide DOWN', 'Now you crawl THROUGH'.

2 The improvised equipment is perhaps even more valuable than the large apparatus. A variety of stout wooden boxes and packing cases gives endless scope for physical activity and for imaginative play. Fifteen or twenty strong wooden trays measuring about 50 × 30 × 10 cm can be built into steps, into a house, into a long train or an aeroplane. Three large packing cases will make two downstairs rooms with a bedroom upstairs. Two or three heavy boxes with rope handles encourage co-operation. Add to these boxes two or three stout planks, an old blanket for use as a carpet, a cover, or even a roof, one or two old car tyres, perhaps even a bench-type seat, and the play possibilities are endless. An empty half-gallon paint tin with a little water in the bottom and an old paint brush—four cm is a good size—makes provision for pretend painting, while a short wooden ladder and a rag are the only equipment necessary for a window-cleaner. If you can find a handy car-breaking yard, you may be able to beg an old steering wheel with about 40 to 50 cm of steering column attached. Drill a large hole with the brace and bit in one of the heavy boxes, and then the column can be pushed through the hole and the box used by bus drivers, fire chiefs, police officers, and captains of boats. If a steering wheel is unobtainable, you can make do with a wooden hoop. Stout cardboard cartons have a short life, but form valuable play material for a few days; the local TV/washing-machine shop may be able to let you have an almost endless supply, but see they are thrown away when they are too tattered for further use.

3 Wheeled toys come next. The supply of these depends not only on cost, but also on the outdoor space available. Unless you have large grounds and plenty of money, tricycles are not a 'best buy': the

left 'how to rub fat into flour' *page 37*

upkeep costs are heavy, they require a lot of space when used freely, and on the whole do not encourage co-operative play. A large porter's trolley that will accommodate several children with a 'strong man' to push them is good value, as are various types of wheelbarrows and carts for carrying loads and encouraging dramatic play. Dolls' prams have already been mentioned as essential. Hobby horses—though not necessarily wheeled, since a broomstick with a sock head is an acceptable substitute—are good play material, though old-fashioned reins for playing horses seem to be unknown to present-day children. Strong wheels are essential for use outside, metal being much more satisfactory than wood, and regular lubricating reduces maintenance costs. This may be the place to mention that the ramshorn hooks of the swing should be regularly greased to prevent excessive wear of the rings: ordinary Vaseline is quite satisfactory.

4 An outside sandpit, large enough for several children to work together, is a great asset. It must have an adequate cover that will keep out the cats, but will also allow free circulation of air to prevent the sand becoming musty. A wide brick, concrete, or wooden surround provides somewhere to sit and somewhere to turn out sandpies. An outside water tray is useful for the warmer weather, but should not be used on cold days, when water play should be confined to a warm room. A patch of earth for digging, and finding worms, spiders, etc. provides the additional contact with natural materials that is so often missing in modern urban life. You may like to combine this digging area with gardening—sowing seeds, planting bulbs, even growing vegetables if you have enough space.

5 In the better weather you can move out into the garden much of the indoor equipment, but do be thoughtful about it. No one can paint if the wind is continually blowing the paper, clay soon becomes unusable if left in the hot sun, the book corner should be put in the shade when the sun is very bright, while jigsaws are probably better left indoors, for it is easier to find the missing piece on the floor than in a flower bed!

When you are arranging the outdoor apparatus, try to leave a clear stretch for running, kicking balls and pushing trucks very fast.

Remember the children's needs for dens and little private houses, and that, as indoors, so outside, play that has 'got stuck' can be opened out and encouraged to develop by a new arrangement of the equipment.

At the end of the session the children can help with the clearing up, but be careful not to clear up too early, or they will be running wild with nothing to do. If possible, do not dismantle an interesting construction that may well be added to next day, but if it is not possible to leave it untouched, perhaps because the premises are used in the evening, draw a quick sketch and then help the children to reassemble it when they return to their play.

6

The Interest Corner

It is difficult to know what descriptive title to give the table or shelf
which accommodates the frequently-changing display of items
brought by you or the children for everyone's enjoyment. Possibly
'the display table' is the most appropriate, but I hesitate to use a
phrase which could give the impression that the items set out were
only there to be looked at, and were not to be handled, discussed,
experimented with. In this chapter I hope it will become apparent
what I mean by the 'interest corner'. At one time it was considered
essential to have a 'nature table', which held a varied collection of
live, dead, and inanimate objects whose only connection with each
other was that they had been produced by some natural rather than
by some mechanical process. Thus, sheep's wool gathered from a
hedge was 'in', a length of homespun wool was possibly 'in', but a
finished skein from the factory was definitely 'out'. It was later real-
ised that objects grouped round a theme were of far greater value,
and it was allowable to display not only pebbles and seaweed, dead
crabs and smelly starfish, but also fishermen's floats and samples of
netting, together with information books about fishing, ships, and
marine life. Then we moved on to the 'discovery table', where an
electric circuit wired to a torch battery, a magnet with a collection
of objects that it could attract, and some that it could not, an old
clock, and even a set of dentures were set out for the children to
handle and to experiment with. We have now reached a more
rational compromise: the display is related to current interests, to the
seasons, to some momentous happening in the world. In our corner
we have had 'some of the oldest rocks in the world' brought by
Jamie after a visit to Iona, alongside a collection of pebbles picked up

by Elaine 'in our flats'. We have had pictures of the moon landing, and of Charles crowned Prince of Wales at Caernarvon. We have had a display of pictures of the Lapp people and their reindeer, with some real reindeer moss to handle and wonder at, after a holiday in Lapland, and we have had a large empty crab shell around which a kind of ritual question and answer grew up: 'Where's its eyes? There they are. Where's its mouth? There it is. Where's its legs? Matthew ate them!'

When you are collecting the many different items suitable for an interest corner, you need to be selective about those you keep when their immediate relevance is over. Some hardware items can be stored until needed again: e.g. magnets, if you make certain the keepers are on, mirrors, electric circuits—disconnect the batteries first. Items that are not easily come by when they are needed, such as a bird's nest—or a crab shell—can be put carefully away. Other less valuable objects you need to be ruthless about: pigeons' feathers are expendable, peacocks' are not. When the current interest is over, dispose of them and collect some more later. Those objects you want to keep can well be stored in some kind of filing cabinet, whether this be a nest of drawers bought from an educational firm, or a series of biscuit cartons which will stack neatly, each clearly labelled with its contents. Interesting illustrative pictures should be filed, so that you can quickly lay your hand on that advertisement from a colour supplement showing bees in a honeycomb, or the page from a 'Shell' calendar with a beautiful picture of ammonites.

Whatever you put on display must be kept fresh and attractive, with clean water in the flower vases, growing plants trimmed and watered as necessary, the acorns and chestnuts removed from the aquarium (and don't forget to arrange for the offender to feed the fish with '*real*' fish food), the dust wiped away, and the whole display added to or completely replaced before the children have lost all interest in it. Most of this can be done with the help of the children, but there are times when you will have to set up your display before they arrive, in which case it may be as well to draw their attention to anything new, for most children need to be helped to look, to *see*. You may find it convenient to do this at storytime.

When shopping at Sale-time, look for remnants of material that will make good display backgrounds: a piece of red velvet for the Christmas season, some green and yellow net for the misty colours of early spring, and so on. Remember to look for 'seconds' among the tea-towels: you may find one illustrating shell-fish, or houses, or peacocks, or a London bus, but make sure the drawing and colouring are good. Keep such display material washed, ironed, and carefully stored ready for use.

Sometimes you can arrange a colour display, using objects that *are* that colour, such as an orange, a bunch of marigolds, an orange-enamelled mug, a cellophane toffee-wrapper, but not things inappropriately coloured, such as a cheese-box painted orange. You can also set up a texture display—smooth, soft, rough, or a shapes display, using circular and spherical items, or prickly pointed ones. Whatever you show, encourage the children to look at, to handle, to talk about the things, and also to bring treasures of their own to add to the display, though you may have to be both welcoming and tactful about the treasured item that does not fit in.

What about your own beautiful but fragile treasures that you would like the children to see? Wait till you know your group well. If you have a child like Johnny whose mere presence used to make my equipment fall to pieces, it is better to show your treasure to the group, and then put it out of harm's way where it can be seen but not touched, just taking it down when someone asks to hold it. If, however, your group has learned to handle a fragile object with care, then take the risk of putting it on show, after explaining the care needed.

Livestock

This is not the place to go into details about the living creatures that can easily be kept in nursery school: there is a list of useful books at the end of the chapter.

Goldfish are best kept in a tank rather than a bowl, with one side shaded from direct light, while tropical fish in a lighted tank are attractive but need a controlled environment. Tadpoles, which should be introduced as spawn, can be reared to the miniature frog stage, but must then be released at the edge of a pond: adult frogs and toads must not be kept in captivity for more than a day or so. Amphibians such as water-tortoises and newts need rather more specialised care, especially as the latter are adept at escaping to explore the environment!

A vivarium is useful for small creatures such as wood lice and beetles which the children find in the garden. Stick insects are very easy to keep and their angularity is fascinating. Caterpillars can be kept if you have the correct leaves for their food, but butterflies and moths must not be kept captive, though they can sometimes be induced to settle for several minutes if you put a few drops of honey or sugar water on a large flower head. Snails make interesting 'pets'; like worms they need a damp environment. Children enjoy the movements of birds; these are best seen in flight cages. A single bird will be lonely at weekends; arrange for it to go home to a welcoming home, or keep at least two together.

Small mammals such as guinea-pigs and rabbits can be kept, as can mice, rats and hamsters by those who enjoy them. Remember their need for company and for daily care: they should not be kept in tiny uncomfortable cages, or left untended at weekends.

Visiting pets are ideal, so long as they are accustomed to children and to travelling, but it is better to insist that they visit by prior arrangement with you so that you do not have to worry about incompatible animals.

Growing Plants

Everyone knows about mustard and cress and carrot tops, together with bulbs in the autumn. What else can be grown? What about a runner bean race? Start them early in the summer term with six foot canes alongside: 'Will they really grow as tall as that?' If grown in pots they need to be kept well watered, and they also need to be protected from visiting livestock, especially rabbits. Nibble ate our morning children's bean, to the great delight of the afternoon children. What about a tomato plant? Or a box of grass seed? Try growing a pot of mixed bird seed: 'If we plant grass seed, what grows? Grass! If we plant flower seeds, what grows? Flowers! If we plant bird seed, what grows? ? ? ?' When you sow seeds, keep a few in a transparent envelope, and try also to germinate a few on some damp cotton wool, so that the children can see all the stages. Point out to them how different in appearance the seeds are. Talk about the part played in seed dispersion by animals, birds and wind. Link stories with growing things: 'My Naughty Little Sister and the Bottle Tree', 'The Tale of a Turnip'. Keep a magnifying glass in the interest corner so that the children can see and wonder at details too small to be noticed without its help.

House plants make the room attractive, but see they are well cared for. Encourage the children to help with watering them and with sponging the leaves. Cut flowers should be put in a vase, not jam-jars, and filled with fresh water when necessary: remember to throw them away when dead, and don't just leave it for Friday afternoon. Bring in leaves, twigs, autumn berries, but do make absolutely sure they are not poisonous. If there is any doubt about this, leave them at home. The same ruling applies to fungi, though you can make an attractive display of even the poisonous varieties in a glass tank with the lid *sealed* on. Use this opportunity to talk to the children about poisonous berries, etc.: I teach mine always to ask before they eat.

Scientific Interests

You will want to 'cash in' on these interests as they arise in the course of a normal day. For instance, a windy day leads to the observation of clouds and smoke, but also to the making of windmills and kites, a trip to see the weather-vane on the church, listening to wind and storm music, and some poems about wind. The feel of the wind in his hair and the sound of it in the chimney will teach a child something real about the weather, but just to put an 'appropriate' symbol on a weather chart is a dull and sterile thing—and how do you decide whether a day is cold or windy or wet when there is room for only one symbol to represent a real February fill-dyke day? Why does it rain? What happens in a country where it does not rain? How much rain falls? Four-year-old Sarah made a rain-gauge and kept a note-book about it, dictating her notes to her teacher. What happens to rain when the sun shines? Leave out a saucer of water to discover evaporation, but protect it from marauding cats and sudden showers, as both spoil the experiment. What happens to plants that get no light, no water?

Every child has his own piece of scientific apparatus: his body. Why, how do we breathe? What happens when we cut ourselves? What are we made of? Use this opportunity to reassure nervous children about cuts and scratches, because their panic may be due to the fear that *all* their blood will escape. What about the heart? The digestive system? Growth and repair? 'The proper study of mankind is man'. Try to get hold of some X-ray photos and display them against the light. Have a reference book that shows the development of a baby, but do point out that limbs develop at the proper time, so that an expectant sibling does not worry, as Matthew did, about his baby having no hands. Be prepared to be misunderstood, however careful you are, and do not give more information than a child is seeking at that particular time, or he will be both confused and bored.

Nursery school science is not all talk: there are many things that you can do. Provide some balloons and a balloon pump, but keep an eye open to ensure that a child, taking a big breath to blow up a balloon, does not suck one into his windpipe. Does a big balloon float higher than a small one? Blow some bubbles and watch them float away. Where do they go when they burst? It is fun to blow bubbles from the top of the climbing frame—they will float away over the fence or over the roof of the school.

MAGNETS are 'magic' to most three-year-olds, and of great scientific interest to four-year-olds. Try to provide bar, round and horseshoe magnets, and also magnetic fishing and perhaps a little train whose carriages are linked by magnets. Keepers must be kept on magnets when not in use; if they are mislaid, an ordinary nail can be used instead.

MIRRORS are of great interest and can be presented in several ways. A wooden block about 15 cm long, with a groove at each end to take two small handbag mirrors, and a small car or other toy to stand between, will give an infinite number of reflections. Turn the block over and put two grooves at an angle to each other across the block near the centre: how many cars can you see now? Buy a reversible shaving mirror in one of the multiple stores: one side will be magnifying. Small round concave and convex mirrors can be bought; if mounted on pieces of plywood they are easier to hold. 'Look at yourself in here. And now in here'. If possible, have a full-length mirror fixed in a suitable place.

TIME is both mysterious and fascinating. A large clear calendar, with birthdays ringed, should be placed where the children can count the days. There should be a clock in the room, with arabic not roman numerals, and you can also provide a clock, either a toy one with movable hands or one no longer in working order, to stand beside it, with its hands pointing to the time of the next activity. The idea of yesterday and tomorrow is very difficult for pre-school children to grasp. 'Do you know where I went tomorrow?' is typical of many such confusions. Answer in the spirit of the question whilst tactfully correcting the mistake. 'No, I don't know where you went yesterday. Tell me about it'. Talk about the names of the days: 'It's Tuesday today: what was yesterday called? What will tomorrow be called?' Think how you will answer the desperate question, '*When* will it be tomorrow?' The names of the months can be introduced via birthdays, festivals and holidays. History is unexpectedly fascinating to some children; they talk about the 'olden days', particularly with reference to cars, trains, etc. Three-year-old Edward suddenly rushed out of the paddling pool to throw his wet arms round my knees and inform me, 'The Black Prince was called Edward. He won battles'. Some young children have a very real interest in dinosaurs, whilst four-year-old John knew more about ammonites than I did.

ELECTRICITY. Set up a simple electric circuit on a board. Buy a small torch bulb and a holder to fit it, a single cell battery and some flex. Screw the holder to the board, having drilled a hole for the flex. Attach the flex to the holder, and fasten the other end of one strand to one terminal of the battery: this can be done satisfactorily with insulating tape—or with sticking plaster from the medical cupboard! Leave the other strand free, with the insulation stripped back a little way so that the wire is exposed. Show the children how touching the other battery terminal with the wire makes the light go on. Make it a little more complicated: fix your bulb holder in the same way, but have two batteries, a single cell and a double. Fix a lead to one terminal on each. Leave the other lead free to reach both the second terminals: see what happens when the lead is touched to the single cell terminal; what when it touches the double. Again, wire a battery to a simple switch—a never-failing attraction, this, but teach the children to leave the light switched *off* unless you are willing to buy a new battery every day. Introduce a problem: wire the bulb directly to the battery, but cut the flex, leaving a gap, with both ends showing exposed wire. Provide a selection of metallic and non-metallic objects. Which of these will bridge the gap and make the light come on? Remember to stress that electric batteries and torches are fun to play with, but that electric current is dangerous; warn the children against interfering with power points and switches.

TEMPERATURE. Provide a room thermometer and also hang one up outside. Which is hotter, indoors or out? A maximum/minimum thermometer is fascinating to children who understand the significance of the movement of mercury in the tube. Show a clinical thermometer, but allow its use only under strict supervision, because of the danger of swallowing broken glass or mercury if it is accidentally bitten.

For further ideas about scientific interests refer to such books as the Ladybird Junior Science series, but do not drift into the position of demonstrator: the emphasis must always be on things that the children can observe and do.

LIST OF 'SCIENCE' BOOKS

Animals as Friends, and How to Keep Them by Margaret Shaw and James Fisher, *published by Dent*

A Zoo on your Windowledge by Joy Spoczynska, *published by Muller*

Animals and Plants: Nuffield Junior Science Source Book, *published by Collins*

See How They Grow series, *published by Nelson*

Let's Read and Find Out Books *published by A. & C. Black*—to help in identification

Young Naturalist Series *published by A. & C. Black*

7

Books

Such an important subject demands a separate section, however brief.

Choosing Books

Choose only those books that are well printed on good quality paper, and are well illustrated. Children should be exposed to the work of good artists, but you must remember that it requires a maturity not attained by all under-fives to perceive in the riotous colour of some modern children's book illustrators the object or the situation illustrated! The illustration should fit the page, so that the children are not puzzled by half an engine or a man with no feet, and there should be only one picture to a double-page spread, so that they are not confused by seeing, for example, two tigers, when the story is about one, because for children of this age pictures are reality, and anything depicted in them is actual, not imaginary. Books need to be strongly bound, preferably stiff-covered, and should open flat so that they are easy to handle and to 'read'. These points refer to the ideal, but it is sometimes worthwhile choosing a book that does not conform in minor details.

Categories of Books

a STORY BOOKS. Those put in the book corner must have illustrations that will enable a child to follow the story from the pictures. The story itself must be worthwhile: good examples are 'The Tiger Who Came to Tea', 'The Little Old Man', and the 'Topsy and Tim' books. Try to include stories of all types of children, homes and backgrounds.

b PICTURE BOOKS. The emphasis here is on the illustrations, not the story that they tell. Include some of artistic value, some dealing with everyday life in the home, in the street, in the country, some about animals and birds, both wild and tame, and also a few very simple picture books for the youngest children. Alphabet books are included in this category.

c NURSERY RHYME BOOKS. There are many good collections available; select not only some of the smaller ones which can be handled easily by the children, but also one or more comprehensive illustrated collections.

d REFERENCE BOOKS. These should have very clear illustrations and information in simple language. Since it is almost impossible in a small school to cater for every topic that may arise, remember that you can turn for help to the children's section of your local library. A one-volume well-illustrated encyclopedia is enjoyed by the older children and leads to a good deal of discussion and questioning, while a small uncomplicated atlas supplements the information obtainable from a globe.

e STORY COLLECTIONS are not provided for the book corner, but some are necessary for your own use.

Book Presentation and Storage

A folding book case with narrow racks which enable the fronts and not the spines of books to be displayed is useful, because it can be opened out to screen off the book corner, but can be folded out of the way when the space is needed. A table large enough for at least three children to read together, and some comfortable chairs are also necessary, or you can provide a low seat, and some cushions on the floor. Good natural lighting is desirable, but if this cannot be arranged, see that the artificial lighting is satisfactory.

There is no need to display all your books at once, indeed it is better to have several sets, each with perhaps fifteen or so books of all types, which can be put out in rotation, the sets being changed in the middle of the week. Any book not out should be supplied on request: at one time 'The Ambulance' had a permanent place on our book rack because Jimmy had to read it first thing each morning before he could settle to anything else. In the same way, William Stobbs' 'The Three Bears' had to be instantly available during Lucy's first few weeks at nursery school.

Reference books can be kept together on a convenient shelf, and the children encouraged to find for themselves the book which will tell them what they need to know. Sometimes the teacher will produce a relevant illustration to help a discussion or to widen a play situation.

Book Maintenance

Children need to be taught how to handle books: how to hold them, how to turn the pages, how to put them away after use. They will be helped to take care of them if the books are kept in good condition by carefully mending small tears, by putting the dust covers in plastic book jackets or covering the board covers with transparent adhesive plastic, and by taking away any that are dog-eared or dirty. Do not make the mistake of giving them only old tattered books 'until they have learned to take care of them'—they will never learn that way. On the other hand, it would be reckless to put out several expensive books for a group that had had no chance to learn book care. Provide first some bright, clean, attractive but relatively inexpensive books, and then later, with due ceremony, put out at first just one 'special' book, gradually adding more as the children become more responsible. Some of the new paperback reprints are ideal for this preliminary learning, particularly if you stiffen the covers with card, and strengthen the spines.

Sources of Books for Children

a Get advice from the children's librarian at your local library.
b Write to the National Book League, 7 Albemarle Street, London W.1.

c Go to any good bookshop with a children's section.

d Take out a subscription to one of the specialist publications. Here are particulars of three:

Growing Point
Mrs. Margery Fisher, Ashton Manor, Northampton.

Books for Your Children
14 Stoke Road, Guildford, Surrey.

Children's Book Review
Five Owls Press Ltd,
67 High Road, Wormley, Broxbourne, Herts.

Attached is a very short list of a few of the many books that are specially enjoyed in my school. It could form the basis of a collection to which you would add others that you had 'discovered', and some of the many new titles that appear in the publishers' lists.

Picture Story Books
Adamson, J. & G.: The 'Topsy and Tim' Books, *Blackie*
Ardizzone, E. & A.: The Little Girl and the Tiny Doll, *Longman Young Books*
Beckmann, K.: Susan Cannot Sleep, *Wheaton*
Bright, R.: The Friendly Bear, *Macmillan*
Brown, M. W.: On Christmas Eve, *Collins*
Flack, M.: The Story about Ping, *The Bodley Head*
Freeman, D.: Dandelion, *World's Work*
Friskey, M.: Indian Two Feet and his Horse, *Muller*
Hertz, G. J.: Lena and Lisa Have Measles, *Burke*
Hoban, R.: Bedtime for Frances, *Faber*
Hughes, S.: Lucy and Tom's Day, *Gollancz*
Hutchins, P.: Rosie's Walk, *Bodley Head*
Keats, E. J.: Peter's Chair, *Bodley Head*
Kerr, J.: The Tiger who came to Tea, *Collins*
Krasilovsky, P.: The Cow Who Fell in the Canal, *World's Work*

'Tools must be real tools' *page 30*

Lindgren, A.: Christmas in the Stable, *Brockhampton*
Locke, E. R.: The Red Door, *World's Work*
Makower, S.: Samson's Breakfast, *Methuen*
Mahy, M.: The Lion in the Meadow, *Dent*
Mamlok, G.: The 'Candy' books, *Nelson*
Marino, D.: Buzzy Bear Goes South, *Brockhampton*
Olsen, A.: Bernadine and the Water Bucket, *Abelard Schuman*
Parish, P.: Willie is My Brother, *Gollancz*
Petersham, M. & M.: The Box with Red Wheels, *Macmillan*
Sandberg, I. & L.: Anna and the Magic Hat, *Sadler Brown*
Slobodkina, E.: Caps for Sale, *World's Work*
Stobbs, W.: The Story of the Three Bears, *Bodley Head*
Worthington, P. & S.: Teddy Bear Coalman, *Warne*

Nursery Rhyme Books

Lines, K.: Lavender's Blue, *Oxford University Press*
Montgomerie, N.: This Little Pig went to Market, *Bodley Head*
Reeves, J.: The Merry-go-Round, *Puffin Books*

Fingerplay Rhymes

Grice, M.: One, Two, Three, Four, *Warne*
This Little Puffin, *Puffin Books*

Information Books

Black's Children's Encyclopaedia, although produced for older children is very useful for reference, and is well illustrated.
The Young Specialist Looks at . . . , *Burke*
Mollie Clarke: Observe and Learn series, *Wheaton*
Things I Like, *A. & C. Black*

Collections of Stories for Telling

Ainsworth, R.: Lucky Dip, *Puffin Books*
Berg, L.: Little Pete Stories, *Puffin Books*
Colwell, E.: Time for a Story, *Puffin Books*
Edwards, D.: My Naughty Little Sister, *Puffin Books*
Sutcliffe, J.: Jacko and Other Stories, *Bodley Head*

'to follow the story from the pictures' *page 51*

8

Language and Storytelling

As a nursery school teacher you have a very important part to play in helping your children towards a rich language experience, and so I think it is useful to be reminded of the nature of language and of the foundations on which it is built.

The Nature of Language

There is a growing tendency to use the term 'language development' when what is really meant is the acquiring of grammar and a vocabulary! I regret this and would like to try and differentiate between speech, vocabulary, communication and language suggesting the following:

a *Speech*: the uttering of words, not necessarily meaningfully.

b *Vocabulary*: the body of words and phrases that is used meaningfully by the speaker. Grammar may usefully be included here.

c *Communication*: the desire to share an experience with another. This may be silent; spoken; written; visual; or tactile. Whichever means is employed, communication is essentially two-way, requiring a 'listener' as well as a 'speaker'.

d *Language* embraces all of these and may be considered from many aspects:
Cultural—national, class, arts/sciences.
Poetic, including the poetic use of words in prose, but not mere verse, which is akin to vocabulary.
Creative.
Scientific.

Rhythmic, including well-balanced sentences, traditional skipping chants and suchlike.

How 'Language' is learned

Speech is learned by imitation, largely unconsciously: hence the importance of deaf babies wearing a hearing-aid, and of the children of deaf-and-dumb parents mixing with normal-speaking children and adults. The child who does not speak at all needs specialist help as early as possible.

Vocabulary is largely dependent on the sub-culture to which the child belongs, and is usually picked up unconsciously, but sometimes deliberately, from the people with whom the child is in contact. The town child may know the noun 'combine-harvester', but is unlikely to include it in his conversation, whilst the country child will speak casually of 'the combine' but remain almost totally ignorant of 'bingo' and 'trolleybuses'. One London nursery school draws its children from a wide variety of social backgrounds: two children were arranging a home corner party, and one was heard to say, 'I'll just pop up to Fortnum and Mason's for some of their special savouries', to which the other replied, 'And I'll just go round to the pub for the beer'.

Communication is the normal thing between young children, and does not entirely depend on understanding what is said. I once watched two boys, just two years old, who sat together at a table, and carried on a real 'dialogue' in their individual jargons, none of which was intelligible to an adult! In the same way, children of different nationalities will play together, even though they cannot understand each other's language. The child who does not want to communicate has an emotional rather than a language disability.

Language is better 'caught than taught' at this age. Talk to the children naturally, read them stories and poetry, tell them about your home life, your out-of-school interests, your own childhood, talk to them about their homes, about what they are doing in school, sing old and new folk-songs to them, point out different accents if you have children or adults from other parts of the country, talk about foreign languages, foreign songs, etc. Discuss figures-of-speech, use and make up metaphors and similes, find all the shades of red in the room, use onomatopeia. Introduce them to the variety and subtlety of their language, making it gay, exciting, expressive. Talk about the 'language' of gesture, of facial expression, let them pretend to be cross, to be frightened, to be fierce. When you read a story, talk about the endpapers, the author, the publisher: why do we write, why do we draw, why do we read? And what about the telephone? Remember that language is part of living.

I now want to consider briefly the development of communication and language in the pre-school years. We all know the primitive means of communication used by the young baby—waving arms, crumpled face, piteous wail, and furious bellow. In the context of the mother/baby relationship these are adequate, but as the child matures, his needs become more complicated and his relationship with his mother more truly personal, and so his mode of communication must become more articulate. A pitiful wail can tell his mother that he is lonely or hungry or uncomfortable, but he needs something more explicit to explain his hunger for fish-and-chips rather than steamed plaice, his need for *her* attention rather than Grandma's, the supreme importance of wearing his blue pullover and not his red. In addition he can fully satisfy his curiosity, express his ideas, understand his environment only by acquiring an extensive vocabulary. Since as well as an adequate vocabulary, true communication requires a 'listener' as well as a 'speaker', in a home where the mother is too busy, too ill, or too unresponsive to talk with her family, the unfortunate child will not be able to develop a rich language: children from such a background entering school at five years old unable to communicate may never catch up with their more articulate contemporaries.

As well as a willing listener, the child must feel an urge to communicate something, whether this be a concrete experience such as falling downstairs or finding a caterpillar, an emotional experience such as being pushed over or mothering a sick doll, or an imaginative experience such as going to the moon or driving a fire-engine.

Whatever the experience, when he puts it into words and discusses it, the child is helped to understand it, to accept it, to make it part of himself. It may be that words alone will not suffice: on the way to nursery school four-year-old Michael had seen a cat run over. Several times during the afternoon he came to talk to me about it. I listened, explained, tried to reassure. At last he lay at my feet rolling a heavy toy lorry up and down his body while we talked, and he was then able to come to terms with this stressful experience. Verbal facility alone was not enough: he also needed non-verbal communication. In the same way, you comfort a distressed child with a cuddle as well as with words: never forget the importance of affectionate physical contact when dealing with young children, though you will not, of course, impose this against their will.

In any group of children, those with good verbal ability are unlikely to be overlooked, but you must be aware of the child who finds nothing 'remarkable'. Such a child needs help to increase his awareness, his ability to *see* rather than just to glance at. This may be done by making time *every day* to talk with these children, showing them interesting things in the environment, comparing them with other things in their lives, using gesture as well as speech: 'Look, here's an engine, waiting in the station; here's a picture of it pulling the train. It's puffing hard, because it's a heavy train. Can you see all the smoke coming from the funnel. Come and look out of the window: see, there's some smoke coming from that chimney. It's blowing away across the sky like this...(gesture)' With the very inarticulate child it may help to talk about the same thing for several days until a spark of enthusiasm is kindled, perhaps when he sees the same known object in a new setting. Andrew came to nursery school at four and two months after a spell in hospital with suspected lead poisoning. He was non-communicating, withdrawn, showing interest only in water-play. A new toy boat kindled that vital spark of enthusiasm, and from there we progressed to talking about boats, big and little, floating and sinking, wet and dry, boats in books, smoke from boats, smoke from engines, smoke from chimneys, what's inside houses, and so on to everyday life. By his second term he was a lively laughing little boy, who *wanted* to communicate. He

59

needed the help of the speech therapist, but would probably catch up with his age group by the time he was five or six.

Another way of making contact with the withdrawn child is through singing. We can use not only traditional nursery rhymes and songs, but also, using familiar tunes, make up songs about him and what he can see. If he is willing for you to hold his hands or to nurse him, you can also help him to feel the rhythm in his body.

If a child does not speak clearly, or if he seems totally unresponsive, it is advisable to ask for a hearing test to be arranged, but it is important in such cases to continue to talk to the child, simply and naturally, even if he does not at present respond. The shy or withdrawn child needs time to learn both that communication is worthwhile and that speech helps communication, and in this he will probably be helped as much if not more by the other children than by all our efforts.

The development of language is a continuous process, but we may find it convenient to consider it in three stages. The first stage is usually the privilege of the parents, and they help in two ways: by not ignoring either smiles or tears, they make a positive response to the baby's early attempts to communicate, and so encourage further attempts on his part. (This is not 'spoiling' the baby, but is rather helping his growth as a person). Then, by talking to the baby, even when he is too young to understand what is said, by singing to him, and by not isolating him the whole time in his silent cot or pram, they are ensuring that he learns by imitation as he grows up in an atmosphere of communication.

During the second stage, the parents are still of primary importance, but will probably be helped by relatives and neighbours as well as by older siblings. The young child enjoys his growing skill with words, and is helped by hearing familiar objects clearly named: e.g. 'Here is your spoon and here is your plate'. There is no need to insist that he repeats the words, and if you find that he makes up his own words, as most young children do, then let him use *his* word while you use *yours*; he will very soon want to use the correct one. In addition to these brief statements and 'one-word sentences', he still needs to hear ordinary conversation, and to be spoken to in the ordinary way, so that he learns the rhythm of speech. Don't just say 'Sit', as if you were training a puppy, but rather 'Come and sit on your chair'.

The third stage is when the vocabulary is extended and enriched, and speech developed as a means of communication between human beings; this is when the nursery school teacher can make her great contributions. The importance of conversation cannot be stressed too much: you must talk to the individual child and to groups of children about their activities, about your work, about the things going on around. There is no need continually to correct grammar or pronunciation, because it is far better that the child should tell you about his ideas and his plans in faulty speech, than that he should be reduced, like Eliza Dolittle in Bernard Shaw's 'Pygmalion', to 'The rain in Spain falls mainly in the plain' spoken with faultless diction. It is not uncommon for the three- or four-year-old to develop a stammer, because he has more ideas struggling for expression than he can find words to express them with, but most children grow out of it. You can best help by trying to reduce the tension, and by showing you are willing to wait while he tries to say what he wants. Professional help should, of course, be sought if the stammer persists.

Children love to learn new words, and there is no need to be afraid to use them in conversation with them. 'What does arrange mean?' 'Weak is like weak and feeble', (a phrase not previously understood). They enjoy using grown-up words: Frances learned 'actually' and for several days tacked it on to the end of almost every sentence. Peter discovered 'probably', and used it frequently and accurately in his rather unintelligible conversation, while Martin, trying to persuade me to cut something for him said, 'I genuinely can't do it'. They enjoy comparisons: 'I'm as hot as the sun!' and opposites: 'As strong as a lion and as weak as a worm', though the double meaning of some words is confusing. Boisterous Simon thought that the opposite of 'wild birds' was 'quiet birds', whilst three-year-old Alison, whose mother had spoken of getting old, said, 'Never mind, Mummy, you're still quite new now'. By using the traditional nursery rhymes, finger-play rhymes and simple poetry, we can develop the children's awareness of the sound of words; they enjoy

61

rhyming and will enthusiastically help to make up doggerel. Jonathan, aged four, tried to rhyme the name of every child in his group, and was remarkably successful, even though most of his efforts were on the level of 'Shane Cutts has a pain in his guts'. Through language, children are helped both to assimilate and to interpret their environment, and their experiences within it, and storytelling can be valuable here. Matthew had cut up some material belonging to a student living at his house. Without comment, I told 'My naughty little sister cuts out', and he sat motionless, almost expressionless, till the end, when he relaxed with a sigh of relief: some other child had done what he had done, but had been forgiven, and was still loved and enjoyed.

Storytelling

Storytime is an essential part of the nursery school daily programme, and I cannot agree with an arrangement of the day that makes the children choose *either* story *or* music. Stories may be read or told to the children at any time, as and when you can free yourself from other activities, or can find someone else to read to the children. An item of family news, a treasure brought to school, a chance remark overheard—any of these may give the cue for a story, or a child may bring a book from the book-corner with the request, 'Please read it *now*'. It is important to use these opportunities whenever possible, but in addition there should be a recognised time for storytelling, when it is the main activity and the children can listen undisturbed, though they should not, of course, be *made* to come if they are unwilling. This storytime should not be too early in the session, and may well be just before home-time, so long as it is not disturbed by parents arriving or children getting ready for lunch.

When choosing stories for reading or telling, it must be remembered that listening to a story is an emotional as well as a language experience. The story should be within the children's range of experience, it should not be frightening or show an aspect of life that you would not wish to stress, it should build up to a climax, and be satisfactorily rounded-off. The choice of a story being a very personal matter, share with your children only those stories you enjoy yourself. A parent reading to a child at home can use a more advanced story than you can use in school: for example, four-year-old Emma enjoyed 'Alice in Wonderland' read by her mother, and was mature enough to appreciate the humour of it, but it would be a bad choice for nursery school.

When you are making a selection of books and stories, the following groupings are a useful guide:

a stories about everyday experiences.

b stories for special occasions, such as new babies, adoptions, birthdays.

c stories about the seasons and the weather.

d stories about naughty children—but not *too* naughty, or they find it distressing.

e stories to ease children's troubles: e.g. tooth extraction and going into hospital. An American book, 'The Friendly Bear', helped a child whose father was a violent alcoholic. In spite of a loving mother, he was finding the world unfriendly, even cruel. I lent him this book, which was kept for several weeks, because he repeatedly asked his mother to read the story, which helped to reassure him that the world *is* a friendly place.

f stories to help the child overcome his feeling of smallness and uselessness.

g stories to arouse compassion, but *always* with a happy ending.

h amusing stories, but never amusement at the expense of someone else.

There are two groups which should not be included. The first group includes most of the traditional fairy stories, which are better left till the five and a half to six stage. In many of these stories there is a cruel element which is not suitable for pre-school children and which can be really terrifying to a sensitive child. A further difficulty is the magic which forms an essential part of the plot, and which is not understood by these young children to whom so much of life appears magical. Exceptions to this ban are 'Three Bears', 'The Three Little Pigs', (if you are careful about the ending: e.g. the big bad wolf can run away to his own home, thus reassuring those children who cannot bear to think of even big bad wolves being homeless, let alone cooked!), and 'The Gingerbread Man', which can end on the matter-of-fact note that, after all, gingerbread men are made to be eaten.

The other group not included is Bible stories. This is a very difficult subject with under-fives, and is better dealt with at home or in Sunday school. If you are obliged to deal with it in nursery school, you should be very careful to ensure that any books chosen are both well written and well illustrated, and that they do not teach the children anything that they will later have to unlearn. Even stories generally accepted as suitable for all young children can lead to difficulty and anxiety: I have not told the story of Noah's Ark since a distressed four-year-old asked me, 'But what happened to all the people who didn't get into the ark?' A very simple picture book, like Bruna's 'The Christmas Story' or the more comprehensive 'My book about Christmas', by Joan Gale Thomas, will help to provide a background for festivities and carols.

Storytime in nursery school needs careful thought if it is to be a happy occasion looked forward to by the children. Those who do not want to join in should not be obliged to do so, but can be expected to play quietly, or, better still, to go into another room with your assistant. Those who choose to come can be expected to remain to the end and not to wander away in the middle, disturbing the group. It is better to have the story period during the second part of the session, so long as it is not in danger of being disturbed by the arrival of parents or the wheeling in of the dinner trolley. Disturbance is also avoided if the children are reminded to go to the lavatory before they settle down to listen.

When thinking about seating arrangements, both the size of the group and the type of story chosen must be taken into consideration. A ring of chairs gives a cosy enclosed feeling, but prevents the story-teller from seeing every child's expression, with the result that she may miss signs of too great tension which could be relieved by a reassuring smile or a twist to the story, or the puzzled frown, which could be helped by a word of explanation. If, however, an illustrated story has been chosen and the children are to follow the story with the pictures, it is better to have a semi-circle of a few chairs, with cushions or a blanket for the rest of the children so there is room enough for all to sit, and every child has a clear view. If you sit slightly to one side rather than in the centre of the open space in front of the children, all can see when you hold up the book.

The actual telling of the story may be in one of three ways, each of which is acceptable and should be used from time to time. Firstly the story may be read directly from the book, and this should always be done when the language is valuable in itself. A good example of this is the William Stobbs' version of 'The Three Bears': do not paraphrase 'that they might not burn their mouths by beginning too soon to eat it', or 'a little rough or so, as the manner of bears is, but for all that, very good-natured and hospitable'. You will be careful that the stories chosen for reading are suitable in plot and vocabulary; 'Tales retold for the tinies' are not a suitable choice. Even though you are reading, be familiar with your story so that you do not have to keep your eyes glued to the book.

The second way of presenting a story is to tell it. This makes for very close contact of teacher with children: you can watch their expressions, share their emotions, and have your hands free for gestures—to be used in moderation. There is no need to learn your story by heart; it is better to remember its shape and progression: the beginning, which introduces the main characters and sets the scene, then the development, leading to the climax, and lastly a rounding-off for a satisfactory ending. It is important to remember the order of incidents, whether it is a simple narrative like 'My Naughty Little Sister', or a cumulative story like 'The Tale of a Turnip', when the same form of words should be used, as children enjoy the repetition, and often like to join in. Do not overstress the climax, though a slight emphasis is often appropriate: 'They pulled, and they pulled, and they pulled . . . and UP came the turnip'. The end may be reassuring: 'The big bad wolf ran away, far away, to his own house, and never came back any more'; quiet and relaxed perhaps: 'That was another good day', but always definite, final, satisfying; 'And they all had turnip soup for supper'. Each story should be a complete experience in itself—this is not the age for serials, though a series of stories about one character or a group of characters is often enjoyed.

Another acceptable way to present a story is to choose a well-illustrated book and show the pictures as it progresses. It is essential that all the children are able to see clearly, so the group must be fairly small and the pictures large and clear. You should then *tell* the story, turning the pages quietly, so that the children can see the appropriate picture; it may be helpful to point unobtrusively to specific objects, but it is better to leave discussion of the picture until the story has ended. Before or after the story it is valuable to draw the children's attention to the book itself: the dustcover, the endpapers, the title page, perhaps the author and illustrator pictured on the back flap. This may also be a good opportunity to talk about the care of books at home, at school and in the library.

When telling stories you should sometimes listen to the sound of your own voice, which should be pleasant, interesting, audible, but not over-dramatic. It can be a salutary experience to listen to a tape-recording of your story, as it can be to listen to the children 'being' the teacher.

You will find that some children like to join in repetitive stories, and they should be allowed to do so. It may occasionally happen that a younger child in the group, or one who is just becoming aware of the fascination of spoken language, repeats single words or phrases after you; you will probably find this distracting, but it has to be tolerated! This phase does not usually last long, and is often a sign that the child is beginning really to listen to the story. Do not let yourself be led, by a circle of rapt faces, into believing that every child is engrossed in your story! More than one are probably thinking their own thoughts, perhaps sparked off by a chance word or incident, and will suddenly burst in with a completely irrelevant comment. Kirsten, at three, was a fidgety listener until one morning when she sat quite still, her eyes fixed on my face, following every word. At the end she remarked, 'You've got a silver tooth!'

When the story is finished there can well be a brief pause. The children should be encouraged to keep their comments and questions, relevant and irrelevant, until then, unless you can see that a child has misunderstood an essential part of the plot, when you can include a brief explanation or 'recap' in your telling. The group should not be questioned on the story and if there are no comments or discussion, this is a suitable time for rhymes and finger-plays. These may continue the theme of the story, though this is not essential. Any poetry used must be simple, short, and good of its kind—rhyming lines do not necessarily make a poem. When you are introducing a new poem to the group, it is usually best to read it to them, then perhaps talk about it a little, and re-read it. If you then read it again on the following day, some of them may well join in, if invited to do so, though this should not be insisted on. In the same way, finger-play rhymes can be read to the group before you show them the actions.

The story may well 'spill over' into music and movement; this aspect will be explored in the following chapter.

9

Music and Movement

I am not a musician—and this section is written to help other such staff—yet I am convinced that music must always be included in the daily programme. Since in many homes there is a continuous background noise from pop radio and television the children learn *not* to listen, and the nursery school therefore must encourage them, and even indeed *teach* them to listen, and to enjoy and respond to music of many kinds. In addition, the children must be offered opportunities to explore the world of sound, and to create their own rhythms and tunes. They should be helped to respond freely to music, and to express emotions and involvement through movement and mime. It must also be remembered that musical experiences should be available for gifted children like three-year-old Ben who, listening to a recording of Britten's 'Young Person's Guide to the Orchestra', asked his teacher, 'Is that the cor anglais? *Why* can't you hear if it is?' All these musical experiences can be provided in two ways: the informal and the organised. As the informal is the more important for this age group, I shall deal with that first.

Informal Music Provision

THE MUSIC CORNER. This, however small, should be accommodated *in* the playroom, for if it is relegated to another room or the corridor, it is virtually impossible for the teacher to be aware of the children's musical experiments, and to pick up the teaching points that arise in a free environment. These points include such things as pointing out the difference in sound quality between two bell sprays, or in pitch between two drums; demonstrating a firm rhythm for

68

marching; singing an appropriate song or playing part of a record; joining an informal percussion group by clapping, using a percussion instrument, or playing a simple piano accompaniment. All this must be done tactfully, almost tentatively, showing interest without interfering, realising when to hold back because a child is enthralled with sound in his own private world.

THE PROVISION AND USE OF INSTRUMENTS. The instruments provided for the children's use in the music corner need not all be expensive but must be pleasant-sounding and in good condition. Battered tin drums and metal tambourines do not afford a true musical experience, though they should not, of course, be rejected out of hand if brought as a 'musical offering' by a child just beginning to be aware of sounds.

Various instruments can be improvised—there is a useful booklet 'Making Musical Apparatus and Instruments' by K. M. Blocksidge, published by The Nursery School Association—and the children will enjoy helping to make them. Let them use their ears as well as their hands, by providing a selection of 'rattles' to choose from when making shakers: e.g. rice, cotton-wool, pebbles. Things to twang are popular—witness the unofficial use made of the expanding wires of the bookshelves!—and you can provide rubber bands, elastic, string, wire of different lengths and tautness. A makeshift 'guitar' that can be tuned will be appreciated. Two half coconut shells are often provided, two walnut shells are not so common. Improvised drums can be made, and the resonance of various empty containers can be tested.

More conventional musical instruments should be provided when they can be afforded. A record player is very valuable, and the records should be of good quality and in good condition. It may be possible to borrow some from the Public Library or from friends. For use by the children, bell sprays, triangles, a tambourine, one or two drums of different sizes, castanets, chime bars—these are all fairly inexpensive. If possible there should be available a glockenspiel, a good xylophone and a piano. These instruments need not all be displayed at once, particularly if space is limited, but all should be available on request.

Provide some books for the music corner, including a few with pictures of orchestral instruments, and at least one with 'music' in it, because some children experimenting with rhythms and tunes on the piano feel they are not doing it 'properly' unless there is a book on the piano rest. Good drawings or photographs of the instruments provided for their use can be displayed from time to time.

Although the instruments are being used informally you should ensure that they are being used carefully. Too much concentration on technique is not appropriate at this stage, but rough or careless handling should not be allowed, the individual child or the group being taught the correct method. Philip, a lively Spanish three-year-old, was banging the tambourine on the floor; explaining that it made a loud harsh noise because it was the wrong way to use it, I showed the more pleasant sounds made by tapping or shaking it. He replied, 'But I like loud noise!' and so I persuaded him to accept a substitute—in this case a wooden brick to bang on the floor with one hand and a bell spray to shake with the other. Children should also be allowed to play the piano, but may be expected to perform reasonably: giants or thunderstorms may require a heavy bass, but this should not be produced with fists or elbows.

SPONTANEOUS GROUP ACTIVITIES. Informal concerts can take place at almost any time with a few children singing and/or playing instruments round the piano or gramophone. They enjoy choosing the songs or tunes to be played, and also enjoy hearing new ones. Old folk songs like 'Billy Boy' or 'Dashing away with her smoothing iron' have strong rhythms, good tunes, and some repetition in the words to encourage the children to join in. Some modern folk music is also valuable, and the occasional pop record will set all the room a-jigging at their play. Better a rhythmic response with the Beatles than boredom with Bach.

On days when it is possible to work outdoors without disturbing the neighbours, an impromptu 'steel band' can be organised with saucepan lids to tap, an old wash-board to rub a stick up and down,

'Children should be allowed to play the piano' *this page*

and extra sticks to tap on a convenient metal pole. A grand parade is most enjoyable too, the teacher leading with a firm rhythm on the drum or tambourine, and the children following, each with an instrument (conventional or improvised), though Rachel at three always preferred to join in with her dolls' pram. A vocal accompaniment is often suggested—'John Brown's Body' (from Daniel, aged four), 'Who's afraid of the big bad wolf?' (Martin, aged three), 'Baa, baa, black sheep' (Catherine Mary, aged three—the only song she knew), and 'Hush-a-bye-baby' from Rachel, anxious lest her sleeping doll be wakened: there was a new baby at Rachel's home about this time.

SINGING TOGETHER. You must always be alert to opportunities for singing informally with the children. You may use well-known songs to fit the occasion: e.g. 'London's burning' as the make-believe firemen rush through the room; 'Hot Cross Buns' and 'Pat-a-cake' whilst cooking, or 'Humpty Dumpty' to console a child after a tumble. You can also make up jingles to a well-known tune; e.g. 'Cressy has a new dress, a blue dress, a new dress, Cressy has a new, blue dress, she's wearing it today'. This informal singing should be light, unforced, simple and appropriate, and should be discontinued if it becomes apparent that it is an intrusion rather than a welcome addition.

'SOOTHING THE SAVAGE BREAST'
Music can be invaluable in helping the disturbed or the handicapped child. I do not intend to go fully into this, because it is a specialised subject, but will give examples of the way in which children with different problems can be helped. One three year old, silent and withdrawn, never spoke to us, though he appeared to be content and would do as he was asked if his hand were taken. He did not respond to the spoken word, but when, one day, I *sang* to him, his face lit up, showing interest for the first time. For some time we sang a commentary on the activities going on around, until, one day,

Many different groups of people work with pre-school children. A Save the Children Fund playgroup in Liverpool. (*SCF photo*) he whispered, 'Sing it again'. Following this breakthrough, normal speech gradually developed, so that by the time he was five he was talking well, with a vocabulary advanced for his age, and had an outstanding singing voice.

A little girl, about the same age, found it difficult to leave her mother at the beginning of the session, until I discovered that her favourite song was 'Blow the Wind Southerly'. Each day, I asked her to say 'goodbye' and then come and sit on my lap at the piano while I played and sang 'her' song. This went on for some weeks until she gradually became able to say a cheerful goodbye and run off to play.

I have also had a child who, if picked up when in a tantrum, would forget his temper if I waltzed with him while humming 'The Merry Widow' or a Strauss waltz, or if I swung his flailing arms to 'Toreador' or 'The Battle Hymn of the Republic'. There are, however, some children who become more rather than less infuriated if you sing to them, so do be tactful.

Organised Provision

The organised music and movement period is no longer considered an essential part of the daily programme: indeed, there are those who, believing that there is no place for it in present-day nursery school routine, advise that *no* organised provision should be made, and that while children's spontaneous movement and music-making should be encouraged, these activities should never be initiated by the teacher. Whilst agreeing that since children are not obliged to paint or to use clay they should not be obliged to take part in a music period, I believe that even as space is arranged and suitable provision made for creative work, so there is much to be said in favour of providing both time and space for listening and moving to music.

I have found that for both music-making and for movement a reasonably quiet and controlled environment is necessary, and that in our small rooms it is not possible to concentrate on music whilst noisy play is going on; in the garden all but the loudest music is drowned by the noise of heavy traffic. I have also found it necessary to clear away a few tables in order to make sufficient space for those who want to move to the music. The arrangements you make will depend on the size of the room, the number of children and so on, but you might consider providing an opportunity for more organised musical activities towards the end of the session when the messier play materials have been cleared away, with quieter occupations left for those who want them. If you intend to link your music with the story it is obviously better to have it after the story period, but if you have planned to play a record or sing some songs this can be done as well before as after.

GENERAL PLANNING PRINCIPLES

Make certain that you include some music worth listening to, whether it is recorded or sung or played on any suitable instrument. Allow the children to respond in their own way, by singing, by moving, or by sitting or even lying listening quietly; bare feet can be encouraged but not insisted on. Do not isolate yourself behind the piano or stay apparently glued to the gramophone, and do vary your choice of percussion instruments: contrasting perhaps tambour and triangle, chime bars and rhythm sticks. Remember that children need to hear good singing, for they hear so much that is poor on radio and TV; they can be encouraged to join in, and will learn the words most readily from watching your face as you enunciate clearly. Be ready to jettison your plans if necessary and to pick up the children's ideas; keep even your 'planned provision' as informal as possible.

SOME SUGGESTIONS TO START YOU THINKING:

a Introduce three differently pitched drums for the Three Bears and a contrast, e.g. a bell spray, for Goldilocks.

b Discuss with the children the choice of suitable instruments to accompany the story of Teddybear Coalman, and then play it out.

c Sing some cat songs, mime stroking a cat's soft fur, be a cat prowling, washing, sleeping.

d Play a record with a strong rhythm, e.g. Brazilian Beat (Decca) and encourage vigorous movement using all parts of the body. Contrast this with quiet restful music, such as a lullaby.

e Invite a friend to bring an instrument, to talk about it and play it. Prepare for this visit by showing pictures and playing suitable records on preceding days.

Whatever the form of the music period, the emphasis is always on *us*, the teacher and children together. Even if she is sitting at the piano the children should feel that she is still with them, sharing the experience. For this reason, broadcast lessons should not be used in nursery school, though some of the material in them may well be incorporated into the teacher's work with her children. On the other hand, she must be careful not to stifle their spontaneity by always moving with them so that they only imitate her instead of making their own response.

COLLECTING SUITABLE MATERIAL

This section ends with some practical suggestions to help you assemble a 'reservoir' of suitable material.

a (This paragraph may be omitted by the musical!) When listening to music on the radio or at a concert, notice any short passages suitable for nursery school use. Then, if possible, borrow a recording, perhaps from the library and tape the chosen passages. This must be done musically by ending the recording at a 'natural break', and by avoiding background noise and a scratchy tape. You must also make sure that you are not infringing any copyright. Keep a note of:

i The title of the music, the composer, and the performer: children are often interested in these details. After hearing 'Scheherezade', four-year-old Stephen asked 'Can we have that Rip-me-corsets-off music'?

ii Its position on the tape.

iii Possible uses of the music: marching, waking-up, etc.

b Collect pictures of musical instruments and music makers from colour supplements, magazines, old textbooks, etc. Mount and file them.

c On school visits or at educational exhibitions, make a note of useful musical books. Buy some of the booklets used with the B.B.C. broadcasts to schools.

d Try to learn to play a recorder, guitar, mouth organ or ocarina. Improvise some musical instruments.

e When possible, e.g. when on sick leave, listen to the schools music broadcasts, criticise them constructively, and select parts you can use with the children, making a note of these. If you have a tape-recorder, tape some of the music used.

10

Health and Hygiene

There was, formerly, a great deal of stress laid on the importance of eating a balanced diet, and of regularly eliminating the waste products therefrom. Opinions on child-rearing tend to recur in cycles, and in the future, no doubt, tremendous stress will again be laid on this, but at present we are more enlightened and are able to take a better-balanced, less intense view of these matters.

The Nursery School Mid-day Meal

Food represents love, affection, caring.

Food eaten under conditions of stress does not nourish adequately.

The child is an individual at mealtimes as he is at playtime.

These three facts affect the arrangements you make for the meal.

There are two acceptable arrangements; family tables, and buffet service. Family tables are possible if you have not more than ten children to each member of staff, and if the kitchen is able to supply the food in small serving dishes. When the tables are laid for lunch, put several together to provide accommodation for a group of children and one adult; tablecloth, flowers, beakers and a jug of water, individual cutlery and serving spoons are all necessary. The children who will sit at the table may help to lay it after washing with the adult who will eat with them. When all members of the group are ready, the meal can begin, with the adult serving them individually by name, remembering their individual appetites and preferences. She may well serve the meat and let them serve themselves with vegetables: a good rule is that while food served to them may on occasion be left on the plate, any food with which they serve themselves must always be eaten. Encourage the children to try a minute portion of unfamiliar foods, and discourage them from taking unduly large helpings of favourite foods; explain that everyone must have one serving and then those who are still hungry can have 'seconds' or even 'thirds'. With this system there should be no need to use the ridiculous 'No pudding because you have not eaten your dinner', as if appetite were determined solely by the amount of food in the stomach! If the first course has not been finished up it is reasonable not to allow second helpings of pudding, but only if the uneaten food was the child's own choice. Drinking water must be available during the meal; water-play will have given useful practice in pouring.

With 'family tables' the adult eats her meal with the children, as in a family and joins in the mealtime conversation; meals should never be eaten in silence—you are teaching the children to live in the world, not a Trappist monastery. Normal table-manners should be encouraged: 'Please will you pass me . . .', 'Please may I have . . .', etc. and the convention that the second course is not served until everyone has finished his first course should be observed, with the proviso that if one child is unusually slow, you ask him, 'Will you excuse us if we start our pudding while you finish your first course?'

If the conversation is interesting, the children will enjoy sitting and talking after they have finished eating, and it will be no hardship to them to wait in their places until most, if not all of the group have finished their meal. It may be necessary to restrict a little the conversation of very voluble children: this can be done in a reasonable, friendly way, 'Alan, before you tell us any more could you just finish your dinner because it's getting cold' (or 'Cook is waiting to wash up', or 'We would like to start our pudding now').

It is sometimes said that family tables put an undue strain on the adult and do not give her adequate opportunity to eat her own meal. This is not so if the group is not too large and the children reasonably socialised, but if there is a large number of children who need help with the actual mechanics of eating, e.g. how to hold spoon and fork, how to fill the spoon and carry the food to the mouth, how to make a clean plate and keep a clean cloth, the adult may well have to give all her attention to this, and will not be able to eat with them, though it is still desirable that she sit at the table and make the meal a social occasion as well as an 'instruction period'. In some areas, volunteers are welcomed into schools to help culturally-deprived children with language and social development; such volunteers would be invaluable at meal-times, enabling small groups of children to eat with and learn from adults.

Buffet service makes the mid-day meal a more informal occasion, and is probably better than family tables where there is a high ratio of children to adults, but does not permit the 'teaching situation' or the social occasion that arises when they eat together. It is not really suitable where there is a large number of children needing help, but, even so, may well be the only satisfactory way of organising the meal for a group of thirty children with only the teacher and one nursery assistant. The children who have washed first should lay sufficient tables for the whole group; these may well seat six or eight but not more. At one side of the room there should be a long serving table to which each child comes to receive *his own* meal from *his* teacher. She may either serve the meat and encourage him to serve himself with vegetables, or she may serve him with a little of everything, whilst inviting him to choose how large a portion he would like; e.g. 'I'll give you some of this meat—it's lamb today—and now some potato. Do you like peas? And tomato?' If he tells you he does not like any item, you can say, 'Then I'll give you a very tiny helping, just to taste. You might like it if you try it today'. You will realise there is not time to spend very long on each child: if you give only one minute to each it will take you half-an-hour to serve thirty: but do avoid slapping the food on the plate and thrusting it at the child because there is a queue building up behind him. If you arrange that the children wash a few at a time and come for their meal as soon as they are ready, you will find that you are able to serve individually without feeling too harassed. When your assistant has finished in the bathroom, she may well start serving the pudding to those who are ready for it. Make no mistake—it is not easy for two adults to get thirty children washed and fed whilst not allowing hurry and tension to disturb the meal, but it *can* be done, with practice and a willingness to experiment in finding the best procedure for your particular circumstances. It helps if you arrange for the slow eaters to start their meal first; this should be done not as a reproach but simply as an acknowledgement that some people eat more slowly than others. It also helps if you put at one end of the room some quiet activities for those who are waiting to wash, or who have finished their meal. Children should not be sent unsupervised into the garden to play.

To return to those three facts given at the start of this section: Food represents love, affection, caring: the National Union of Teachers rightly insists that teachers should not be obliged to supervise school dinners, but you, as a nursery school teacher, are in a different position: you must not 'opt out' of the mid-day meal, which is part of the nursery school day, and cannot be left to the assistant and the 'dinner ladies'. Food eaten under conditions of stress does not nourish adequately: I have discussed ways of serving the meal to keep down the tension, relax the pressure, and make the meal a happy social occasion.

The child is an individual at mealtimes as he is at playtime: you will remember to respect his likes and dislikes with regard to food, and to be tolerant of his rate of eating. NEVER force him to eat—an interested but unemotional attitude on your part will do more to dispose of any food fads.

A word of warning: you may have in your group a child with an allergy to certain foods. Make certain that all your staff know of this, and, in addition, make certain it is written down somewhere for easy reference by any person taking your place during your absence.

CLEARING UP

Children enjoy clearing the tables. At family tables the plates can be passed round and stacked together; with buffet service the children will bring their empty plates to a table near the serving table, and should be taught to scrape any scraps into a container before putting the plates into a pile and the cutlery into a bowl. At the end of the meal, beakers should be brought to the table, and cloths and flowers removed; this can, of course, be done by the children. Do see that the slowest eater is not left at a bare table from which everything has been removed, though if slowness is delaying everyone, he can be asked to move to the end of the room with his table, etc.; he should sit where he can see the others, not in isolation with his back to the room.

Unless the children are exceptionally skilful there will be some mess on the floor at the end of the meal. This should be picked up, and any patches wiped with a damp cloth, but the floor should not be swept while anyone is still eating, or if the room is to be used for the rest period, as sweeping disturbs the dust. Before the children rest, they should go to the lavatory, wash their hands, and, if necessary, wipe their mouths.

The Mid-session Milk

In the full-day school milk is more often served once, usually in the afternoon. You can arrange for this to be done informally, the bottles or beakers being on a table at the side where the children can take their own as they are ready. They should be expected to sit down, or at least to stand still, and to drink *slowly*—milk should never be gulped down. Milk should also be served informally in the half-day school. Your nursery assistant can put out a table in any suitable space, and the children can lay the cloth, etc., the flowers and the container for straws. You will probably find that the 'suitable space' is not always in the same part of the room; this does not matter at all. Use whichever space happens to be free at the time, and avoid disturbing the children's activities. If your assistant puts the milk near the table, together with a receptacle for used straws and bottle tops, the children can come and have their milk in between their activities. They should be taught to sit down and to drink slowly; if biscuits and apple or carrot are provided, they should be eaten in that order. Do make sure that in her anxiety to 'get milk finished and cleared away' your assistant does not interrupt the children's play, though it is quite in order for her to ask a child, 'When you have finished that, will you please come and have your milk before you start anything else', and then perhaps to leave the last two or three milks at the side if the children are still not ready to come for them.

Drinking Water

Drinking water should always be available for the children, and should be drawn from a mains tap. If there is a drinking water tap in the bathroom a supply of clean beakers can be kept nearby; if not, there should be a jug of drinking water, covered with a cloth, and some beakers readily accessible in the playroom. Teach the children to put used beakers in a different place from the clean, so that you are sure that each child drinks from a clean cup—and do not make the mistake I used to make of referring to a used cup as a dirty one, because they may assure you that it is not dirty, but clean, and will turn it around to prove to you that they were quite correct to put it back with the clean ones! A child who drinks an unusually large quantity should be referred to the school nurse or doctor for checking against possible diabetes, and the parents consulted.

The Rest Period

In the full-day school it is reasonable that the children should spend half an hour quietly after the mid-day meal: it is not reasonable that they should be expected to sleep. I would also think it reasonable that the teacher be entitled to a peaceful period, though opinions about this differ.

If a rest bed is provided for every child, then every child can be expected to retire to his own bed, decorated with his own symbol, for the rest period, but should be allowed to take with him the toy of his choice—a book, a puzzle, a car, a doll, etc. A short period of quiet, say fifteen minutes, may be insisted on, to allow children who are tired to go to sleep. Restful music can be played on the gramophone, but I would not recommend well-known songs, which encourage too much audience participation. The children will probably be lying down during this quiet time, perhaps playing with their chosen toy, but not making 'social contact' with their neighbours. The pressures of group life are tiring, and a break is good for all. You will sit quietly, perhaps by a child's bed, if he is new or disturbed or restless, perhaps in a comfortable chair with your feet up. Remember that children associate bed time with their mothers, so do not expect any child to stay for rest until he knows you well enough to be able to relax happily on his bed. It is better to refer to this period as rest rather than bed time, while the term 'daybed', though not strictly accurate, may be more acceptable than just 'bed'. 'Stretcher' is used in some schools, but might have unwelcome connections for some children. You will find that some children *need* to sleep, and so the period must be peaceful enough to allow them to do so. Poor housing conditions usually result in disturbed sleep, whilst emotional stress may also prevent a child enjoying a good night's rest as in the case of a three-year-old who, sleeping badly at home because of her mother's great anxiety about her husband's dangerous illness, told her mother, 'But I'll have a good sleep at school because it's all right there'.

After the initial period of quiet you may like to read a story to those who are still awake. This should be peaceful rather than exciting, and may well be slightly more advanced than a storytime story. I have used the Milly-Molly-Mandy stories as a rest time series, and a friend has found her children enjoy Winnie-the-Pooh.

The beds should have washable sheets tied over the canvas slings; these should be changed weekly, sent to the laundry and, when returned, checked for tears or missing tapes. It may be possible to arrange for a rota of mothers to come in to do the sewing, but if not, your nursery assistant will deal with it. Blankets must be adequate, and if the children sleep out-of-doors they will need extra thick ones in cold weather. Care should be taken that blankets are not allowed to drag on the ground, getting dirty or damp, and although the children can be expected to 'tidy' their beds, they should not be required to fold blankets that are too large and heavy for them to manage. In very cold weather the children should sleep indoors, because they may become chilled if, when they wake, they crawl out from a warm cocoon of blankets and sit shivering in the cold air while they struggle sleepily to put on their shoes. The room should be well ventilated even in cold weather while the children are resting; you may be glad to put on an extra woolly, or even to wrap yourself in a spare blanket. If the children sleep outside in the summer, be certain they are in the shade for the whole period. The position of shade varies considerably even in half an hour, so this must be kept in mind when the beds are put out.

Occasionally children wet their beds during the rest period. If this happens the sheet should be changed and the canvas sling scrubbed, and put out to dry *and air*. It is not usually possible to wash the blanket, but the wet patch can be sponged or rinsed with tepid water. Some children tend to pass water just as they wake, and it may be possible to 'catch' them if you are watchful, but this must be done *gently*. No child still half-asleep should be dragged unceremoniously from his bed and sent tottering to the lavatory with the instruction, 'Be quick, before you wet yourself'. Persistent wetters may have a plastic sheet covered with some absorbent material. Do not make too great an issue of this or you will create such an atmosphere of tension that the situation worsens, and the child experiences a feeling of failure and rejection about something quite beyond his control.

In the part-time school you will not need to include a rest period in the daily programme, but it is good to arrange for any child who is tired or somewhat 'under the weather' to have the opportunity to lie down quietly, and perhaps to sleep. A child who has had a bad fall or who is showing signs of shock following some accident should always be encouraged to lie down. I have found that the provision of a 'daybed' in the home corner and in the hospital corner has many practical advantages: not only does it add considerably to the value of the play material provided but, in addition, the beds are kept aired by being in constant use, and are a familiar restplace to the child who needs to lie down. It is better to move the bed from the house or hospital, asking leave to borrow it from its temporary occupant, whether it be Dad sleeping after the night shift, or Mary in hospital with the measles, and put it in a quiet corner, explaining to the resultant crowd of onlookers that John just needs to rest a little while because he has hurt his head, so 'would you play quite quietly until he feels better', or just that Lucy feels very tired because she went to bed late last night after going to the circus. A child who obviously needs to rest, but who is unwilling to lie on a bed, may be glad to curl up in an armchair, wrapped in a blanket, and with a favourite toy to hold, particularly if you are able to bring a chair from the office or staff-room, thus making it easy for him to indulge his need to 'cuddle down', because everyone can see he is not a baby, as he's in a grown-up chair!

It would be a mistake to think that children can only rest in bed or curled up in a chair, for many will, after a spell of vigorous play outside, come in and flop down in the book corner, possibly turning over the pages of a book without really looking at them. This is a good time for an adult to offer to read to a child, perhaps taking him on her lap so that he can relax comfortably and recharge his batteries. Some children find jigsaw puzzles restful; there is great satisfaction in breaking up and then repairing the damage, in bringing order from disorder. Other children may rest on the swing or the rocking-horse, or by crawling into a box or under a blanket. Dan, as a three-year-old, used to like to lie curled up on the trolley, completely covered with a blanket, whilst a grown-up pushed him round the garden, but at four he would lie full-length smoking one of his rolled-up-paper cigarettes, completely withdrawn into himself.

As you observe the children, notice any who frequently appear over-tired, and try to discuss them with their mothers. It may be the result of late nights or too much television, or more seriously, of bad housing conditions, anaemia or even kidney trouble, though it is not wise to suggest such causes to the mother; it is better to advise a visit to the family doctor so that he can 'check whether there is a physical cause'.

11

The Child in the Group

Coming to nursery school may be a child's first experience of life with other children; it may even be his first real contact with adults outside his home circle. Such a child will need a great deal of help, which must be given by both parent and teacher; it may also be found that the mother needs help, too.

Gradual Entry

This is the term usually applied to the practice of allowing children to become accustomed to nursery school life over a period of time, and it is extremely important, but as children vary a great deal in their ability to adjust to group life and to unfamiliar adults, no hard and fast rules can be laid down.

Mothers of new entrants should not be expected to leave them at first, though children whose older siblings have attended nursery school are often 'settled in' by the time their turn arrives; they know the staff, and the geography of the building, have usually made a few unofficial experiments with the play material, and have perhaps protested loudly when taken home! Even so, do not make the mistake of thinking that such a child will, of course, have no difficulties: it is one thing to enjoy nursery school when time is limited and your mother is chatting in the background, and quite another to be left to cope alone with a full session. Again, not all children of a family react in the same way: the happy confident girl may have a timid brother who will need a great deal of help when his turn comes.

The child who is completely new to nursery school life may need to visit with his mother on several occasions during the weeks preceding his admission. These visits should be made at various times, so that he becomes familiar with the whole of the daily programme; it is particularly important that he should see the children going home, or he may think that nursery school is a community of orphans, and so be unwilling to join them! Once he has been formally admitted, and his name put on the register, you can discuss with his mother when she will start leaving him for a short while. (In almost every case this can be done without distressing the child). It is not usual for a child to stay in the group without a parent before he has been formally admitted, as local education authorities are normally legally responsible only for children on the register.

Before the mother leaves her child for the first time at school, she should explain to him in this kind of way: 'While you are playing I am going round to the shops to get some bread. I'll only be a little while, and Miss X will be your friend while I'm gone'. When the child has settled to play, she can say, 'Good-bye now. I'm just going to get that bread. I'll see you very soon,' and then GO. Her good-bye should be short and matter-of-fact, indeed prolonging it may well upset the child, but once she has said she is going, she should go, leaving the child with you, even if he is distressed, in which case you will, of course, comfort him in whichever way seems best in the circumstances, whilst reassuring him that his mother will be back very soon, and that you are looking after him until her return. The first absence should be very brief—probably only five to ten minutes —and this may be gradually lengthened each day, but making sure that the child is not put under too much strain, which might result in disturbed nights, bad dreams, loss of appetite, or over-dependence at home. Some children may need to start with a four or even a three day week; some may prove not to be ready for nursery school life, in which case entry may be delayed for some months, and then a new attempt made. We tried to admit Rachel when she was only two years and nine months, so that she would have one term with her sister, but she was too distressed for us to persevere. The following term she told her mother: 'I'm three now, so I won't cry when I go to school', and she came in very happily.

A word of warning. During this settling-in period the child may well find it difficult to know who is, in fact, in charge. His mother may feel uncertain about checking him in your presence, and he will sense this and act accordingly. When dealing with this situation it is of the utmost importance that you do nothing to weaken her authority or her self-confidence and the less of these that she has, the more important it is that you should 'bolster her up'. You may feel it advisable to explain to the child the rule that his behaviour is infringing: e.g. 'Let's put the scissors back on the table. We don't walk about holding them, in case you have an accident. See, Mummy will look after your cutting-out for you', in this way including her in the situation; or you may instead explain the rules to the mother, and ask her to deal with the child 'because you know him so much better than I do'. At all times, show your respect for the mother's relationship with her child and, so far as you are able, be ready to be guided by her knowledge of him.

The Over-dependent Child

There are a few children who at three or even four years old will not willingly let their mothers leave, however long the period of gradual entry. This is usually due to some traumatic experience in early life —perhaps a period of hospitalisation, or the mother's absence from home for some reason. In such cases, discuss procedure with the mother, offering your advice, but always remembering that she has feelings too, and that it is distressing for her to leave a screaming child with the teacher. A practical plan is for her to talk to the child at home, reminding him that he knows Miss X, that he is getting big now, that he knows what goes on at nursery school, etc., and then telling him that on such and such a day she is going out, just for ten minutes, and will then come back to school and take him home. I have found that it is usually best that he should be left for the first time on a midweek day, rather than on a Monday, when he may not have got over the weekend break, or on a Friday, when he is prob-ably tired. When the day comes, his mother should tell him that she is just going to buy so-and-so and will soon be back, and then she should *go*, so that you and she are in charge of the situation, and the child does not have to bear this burden as well. A very nervous child will be helped if she leaves him some personal possession—gloves, a scarf, a bag—as assurance that she will return. During the time she is away, talk quietly to the child—he will hear you even if he is screaming—telling him that you are looking after him, stressing repeatedly that his mummy is coming back soon, and, when he is calm enough, encouraging him to do something to show her on her return. Neither his mother nor you should scold him for being 'naughty', i.e. screaming, or ridicule him for being 'silly'. When she comes back, his mother greets him lovingly, shows him her shopping, admires anything he has done, and then takes him home, thus helping him to realise that mummies come at home-time, and discouraging him from making a fuss so that his mother will return early and then stay to dance attendance on him while he plays!

Warning! When you are trying to comfort the child, do remember that not all children like being picked up and cuddled, particularly by a comparative stranger. He may be willing to hold your hand, but he may not accept even this limited contact, and you should respect his feelings.

The Dependent Mother

You will occasionally meet the mother who is so dependent on her child that it is *she* who cannot settle into nursery school routine! This may be due to mistrust of her own position as a mother, or to other causes, but she will almost certainly be unaware of these things. She may feel that if her child does not cry when she leaves him, then he does not love her, and she will prolong the good-byes, adjuring him not to cry, until he does! She may consciously want him to enjoy the advantages of nursery school, but without knowing it, she may dread the empty house when he is not around, or resent his affection for the teacher. It is not easy to be a mother when your child kisses you, saying, 'You Miss X' as three-year-old Andrew did. His mother took it very well, bless her.

Whatever the difficulty, do not ever tell the mother it is her fault, but help her by showing your admiration for her achievements, by reassuring her of her child's love, pointing out that he can leave her cheerfully only because he trusts her, and by commiserating with her over the difficulties of being a mother. Stress in every possible way the positive side of their relationship, and help her to feel pride in his growing maturity and developing skills.

The Rejecting Mother

There are a very few unfortunate mothers who are unable to accept their children and who, although they may give adequate or even excellent physical care, give no love and affection. This is a serious and deep-seated problem that you are not qualified to deal with. Do nothing to antagonise the mother further against the child. A cheerful greeting to both of them when they arrive, and a matter-of-fact comment on the child's work when they go home are usually the safest, though you may be able, very occasionally, to make a closer approach, for instance like this: 'I thought that you would be interested to see this that X did this morning. He worked very hard at it, and it's really rather lovely, I think, don't you?' You will, however, still have to deal with the child who says, 'My Mum put my painting on the fire', even though all you may be able to say is, 'Oh, I *am* sorry. Never mind, it was fun doing it, wasn't it? Perhaps you'll do one for *me* to take home this morning'.

Dealing with Aggression

Aggression is normal. The child who is never aggressive is in some degree neurotic, for the aggressive drive is necessary in dealing with life. Because of this we need to provide legitimate outlets for this aggression, e.g. climbing activities involving a physical challenge; constructive activities such as woodwork, involving hammering, etc.; malleable materials such as clay and sand for banging and chopping; balls for kicking; and some indestructible soft toys for use as scapegoats. I do not believe that children benefit from un-controlled behaviour in the school situation, though they may of course do so in the Child Guidance Clinic, and I would therefore advocate quite definite limits even for legitimate expressions of aggression. There will, however, be times when his hostility is aroused and he bursts out in some uncontrolled aggressive manner that cannot be allowed.

a Aggression against inanimate objects, such as kicking the furniture, can usually be diverted into some harmless activity. Daniel, when enraged, would willingly go outside and kick the concrete front door step instead of the paint on the play room door. He needed to kick. We appreciated this. Because we were sympathetic, he was reasonable. Another child may gladly accept the offer of a game of football, or a turn with the wooden hammer toy as a substitute for some action damaging to the equipment.

b Aggression against an adult should not be permitted, for the child's own sake: he will be frightened of his power if he is allowed to hurt. There is no need to scold him for 'daring' to hit you, but you can say, 'I'm sorry you're cross, but I can't let you do that'. It may be necessary to restrain him using as little force as possible—it is humiliating for the child to be physically overpowered. If he has completely lost control of himself it is usually easier to restrain him from behind, putting your arms around him and holding his back firmly against you, thus avoiding kicks, blows and bites, but all the while talking gently, calmly, and offering to leave go as soon as he feels better. When the storm has passed it helps to sponge the child's face with cool water, to tidy his hair and clothing if necessary, and to suggest some quiet activity, preferably with you, such as looking at a book or doing a puzzle. If you are able to take the child into another room with you until his tantrum is over, this is good, but if this is not possible, keep him with you in the room, because he will be frightened of his own rage if left to deal with it alone.

One word of warning: the child's aggression may rouse a hidden aggression in you that perhaps goes back to your own childhood. Try to recognise this in yourself, to accept it and control it, resisting an immature urge to hit back. Do not worry that a child's tantrum reflects adversely on your control, for it may be a sign that he trusts you enough to show his aggression. After a tantrum, four-year-old Rachel said to her teacher: 'I wouldn't hit you if I didn't love you'.

c Aggression towards other children must be handled very carefully. Whilst you may recognise the cause of the aggression, you must also insist on the victim's rights. The outburst may be a reaction to some frustration, such as another child accidentally knocking his bricks down, when you can say something like this: 'No, don't hit him, he didn't mean to do it. Look, we'll put it right again. Robert, will you come and help us, because you didn't mean to do it, did you? Is this how it goes, Martin?'

Sometimes aggression is caused by jealousy of another child. There may be no obvious reason for this feeling—perhaps he is reminded of a sibling rival, or perhaps he is jealous of another child's relationship with you, but he seems to seize any opportunity to pick a quarrel. This is when you have to protect the victim without excluding the aggressor. You might say: 'No, you may not do that to Selina. Yes, I know you don't like her and are cross because she has the book you want and she is sitting on my lap, but she is part of our nursery school, and we must be nice to her and nice to you and nice to everybody. You come and sit here beside me and look at the book with Selina and me, will you?'

Frequent aggressive outbursts are a sign of personal strain and unhappiness due, perhaps, to difficult home conditions. Try to keep 'one jump ahead' and forestall these scenes. It may help if you give the child extra attention, or do him little personal services such as putting on his coat or his shoes for him. If you are unsuccessful, and another child is hurt, include the aggressor in your comforting and first aid: 'Look, do you see that bruise where you kicked Belinda? We'll all go into the bathroom together and put some witch hazel on it. There, Belinda, that will soon feel better. Now we'll find the Smartie tin. Belinda, *you* take one to make you feel better because he hurt you. And now *you* take one to make *you* feel better because you were cross'. This may seem to be rewarding bad behaviour, but it is not really so, being an attempt to deal with the cause of the trouble:

I do not think you will find a child who will deliberately kick another for the sake of getting a Smartie.

It is not a good thing to try to make a child 'say sorry' against his will, though he may be willing to if it is suggested tactfully to him. Try to understand that the aggressive child should not be blamed, but rather that he needs your help in controlling his outbursts. Nevertheless, other children must be protected, and it may be necessary to keep the child close by you 'until you feel better and can remember not to hurt the others any more'. This should not be looked on as a punishment, but rather as an attempt to help him.

There are two kinds of aggressive behaviour to which it is better to turn a blind eye, unless it appears that serious damage may be done. The first kind is the fight between equals: this is often a sign of friendship, as Peter, aged four, said when a timid child feared attack. 'I wouldn't hit *him*. I don't even like him'. Even if it is a dispute over some game or toy, they may be allowed to scrap for a short while, after which they will probably resolve their differences and play peaceably together. The other occasion is when the child who is usually the victim turns on his attacker, who may be overwhelmed and in tears at this unexpected onslaught. You will be well advised not to interfere too soon, but help them to reconcile their differences at the end. Be careful you are not *seen* to be watching, since the child who has been unexpectedly attacked will find it unfair that *he* should be 'beaten up' when you do not allow him to 'beat up' others.

In all cases of aggression try to deal with the victim and the aggressor together, because they are both part of one situation. Some children seem to be natural 'murderees' so try to recognise the potential victim in the group, and help to build up a positive personality with something to contribute to the community, and at the same time, try to recognise the potential aggressor, and give him extra attention and affection to help him through a difficult time.

A Word about Biting

This arouses strong emotions in many adults, who regard it as much worse than kicking or hitting. The first thing to remember is that the victim needs comfort and reassurance as well as first aid. You can cuddle the child, saying something like this: 'Oh, I *am* sorry—that *is* a nasty mark. Yes, I'm sure it does hurt, but it will soon begin to feel better. Let's put something soothing on it. Now we'll cover it up, and let's try and make Alistair happy so that he doesn't feel like biting any more'. A child usually bites when he feels unbearably frustrated and unable to find words or actions suitable for the occasion. A persistent biter needs special help, both to find more acceptable ways of expressing emotion and to build up his confidence and help him deal with frustration. There is never a case for biting back or for teaching the victim to do so: it might be effective in stopping the biting, but would do nothing to help the aggressor achieve more positive attitudes.

Naughtiness

Most children are accused at one time or another, at home or at school or both, of being 'naughty'. I would like to suggest to you that 'naughtiness' is a convenient blanket term which includes all varieties of behaviour inconvenient to the adult in charge! Is it 'naughty' to spill the paint, or is it the result of poor co-ordination or over-enthusiasm? Is it 'naughty' to hide a school toy in your pocket, or is it the desire to have at home a tiny part of this lovely experience that is school? Is it 'naughty' to throw a tantrum, or is it a cry for help?

On the other hand, I do not want to suggest that no child is ever naughty, because there is a certain deliberate 'naughtiness' which is a testing of grown-ups in order to find out the bounds of acceptable behaviour, and the results which follow deliberate disobedience. Never warn a child 'If you do that again, I'll do so-and-so', unless you are prepared to carry out your threat when he repeats the action to see whether you mean it! A child who is continually subjected to idle threats only learns that the adult's word cannot be relied on. On the other hand, it would be unfair to punish a child unless he had first been warned, or unless he knew the rule and the penalty for breaking it. If you find you are continually regarding a child as 'naughty', try rethinking your approach. Is he unhappy at home? Is your school routine too formal or too strict? Are you supplying enough physical, enough intellectual activity? Has he some special interest which you can foster, and in so doing find a better relationship with him? If a child is always in trouble at home, you *may* be able to help his parents to handle the situation more wisely, but only if you approach the problem very tentatively and humbly. It is one thing to deal successfully with a child's difficulties in the unemotional school setting where you have him for only a few hours a day, and quite another to deal with the same child at home, day and night, with the beds to make, the dinner to cook, the shopping to do and the innumerable conflicting demands of the other children and the husband to be met. When we are tempted to criticise the shortcomings of parents, we may well wonder whether we would do as well in similar circumstances!

Telling the Truth

There is no clear line in a young child's mind between fact, fantasy, and 'the magic of wishing', and so he should never be accused of lying, or be put in the position of trying to escape trouble by not telling the truth. If you *know* (not just suspect) that a child has committed some offence, rather than asking him whether he did it, it is better to say: 'I am very sorry you did that; you know you shouldn't have done it, don't you. Now we must see what we can do to put it right'. If you do not know who did it, it is seldom helpful to enquire! Deal with a minor offence in a general way, showing the children that although undesirable, it is not a matter for serious concern. For example you might say: 'Somebody has knocked the paste over and not wiped it up, and now it is all over the floor. Frances, would you run and get me the floor-cloth, please, while Joanna picks up the pot and the brush. Thank you so much. Now I will clean it up before it makes any more mess'.

The 'magic of wishing' leads the child to believe that what he wants to be so, *is* so. This is often a form of 'keeping up with the Joneses';

i.e. 'My Mummy loves *me* just as much as your Mummy loves *you*, and so she *must* have bought me some new shoes like yours, and so I can talk about them like you do'. It is seldom necessary to expose their fantasy, and this should never be done in front of other children. You can help a child to distinguish between fact and fantasy by explaining that sometimes we want a thing so much that we like to pretend that we have it, although we know that we haven't really. One cannot 'bend reality' and you should not try to do so for children. On the lighter side, it is sometimes fun to go along with the make-believe, and, when the child tells you that he saw a lion when he was coming to school, you describe in minute detail the alligator with pink stripes and purple spots that *you* saw hiding behind the pillar-box! He will soon notice the twinkle in your eye, and join in the fun.

A Word about Tale-Telling

The young child needs to feel sure of the rules, and he will often come to you with a 'tale': 'So-and-so has done such-and-such', but what he is *really* saying is: 'I thought the rule was such-and-such, but so-and-so did something different. Which of us is right?' The right reply is not, 'Run away and mind your own business: it's not nice to tell tales', but rather, 'Thank you for telling me. Let's go and put it right', thus encouraging him to come and help you. The child who did 'such-and-such' can be gently and firmly reminded that 'We don't do that because . . .,' and be helped to deal with any resulting disturbance of his activity. In this way the framework of order is maintained, and the children feel secure.

There is, however, another kind of tale-telling which should not be indulged in: you should not greet a mother with the tale of her child's misdeeds! What is done wrong at school is dealt with at school, and should not cast a cloud over home-going. Indeed, the more difficult a child's behaviour, the more important it is to emphasise what he has done right and to send him home with a positive feeling of success, however small, rather than with the shadow of repeated misdemeanours. On the other hand, if a child's behaviour is causing you real anxiety, try to discuss it with his mother in private, asking her help and advice as well as perhaps offering yours.

A Word about Swearing

I divide young children's swearing into three groups; the first is 'normal speech'. Children who hear swearing as part of everyday language at home will use it naturally without any idea that it is 'wrong'. As a mother said to me, 'I don't know where he gets his b . . . language from'. These children should not be told it is naughty to say it—this would appear as adverse criticism of the parents which is never permissible in front of the child—but may just be told, 'We don't use those words at nursery school'.

The second group may be termed 'the attempt to shock'. Children pick up words from each other, both good and not so good, and use them at home. A shocked reaction to a swear word may be good fun to the child, and so he continues to use it to provoke interesting reactions! If its use is ignored, it is soon discontinued.

Lastly there is the 'innocent use'. A child may hear swearing without knowing it is undesirable, and so use a word or phrase innocently. He may be gently told, 'That is not a word we use in school (at home). It is better to say . . .', substituting a suitable verb or adjective.

We can be glad that the 'bad old days', when a child's mouth was washed out with carbolic soap and water, are no longer with us, but you may find that parents are glad of advice as to suitable treatment of this problem.

12

Meeting Intellectual Needs

The way you set out your room, the materials you provide, the illustrations you put up and the reference books you display will all influence the children's intellectual development, but it is not sufficient just to provide a stimulating environment; you must both encourage the children to notice, to question, and to explore the phenomena encountered in their use of material, and also supply the necessary information at the time it is needed.

What? Why? How? The child's thirst for knowledge and his search for understanding are frequently expressed in questions beginning with these words, and it is often good to reply with another question in order to lead him to think out the answer. Sarah, aged four, asked one Christmas-time 'Was Jesus the first person in the world?' 'Think, Sarah', said her teacher. 'No, he couldn't have been, because he had a mummy and a daddy. Were they the first people in the world?' 'Think again'. 'No, they weren't, because some people came to visit him'. In the same way, the question 'Why does the paint run down the paper?' is not helpfully answered by telling him that he didn't wipe his brush on the side of the jar. Instead, ask him, 'Does it run if you put your paper flat?' On the other hand, the question, 'What does a real cuckoo look like?' is better answered by an invitation to 'Come and let's find a picture in the bird book'.

While the children are playing, be alert to opportunities to query what is happening: 'What has happened to the water you tipped in the sand?' 'What would happen if we buried a piece of polythene in the sand?' 'Did you see what happened when you painted yellow over blue?' 'Can you think why your castle fell down?'

You want to teach, not facts, but an attitude to learning. It is not important if he confuses a cuckoo with a pigeon, but it is important that he should know that it is possible to find out which is which. It does not matter if he cannot count accurately to twenty, but it does matter if he cannot make a bridge over his railway because he does not know how to make the supporting piers of equal height. Help him to find out what he needs to know at the time, but do not try to feed him isolated information or irrelevant facts.

Reading

If you consider carefully you will find that you do, in fact, include a number of pre-reading activities in your daily programme, and this is as it should be. To name a few: jigsaws give practice in recognising size and shape, labels on pegs help children to recognise their own and their friends' names, the book corner provides opportunities for seeing print, for following stories from pictures, creative work from 'junk' suggests conversation about the printing on boxes and cartons. So why the enormous emphasis that is sometimes laid on learning to read early, even in babyhood? There is absolutely no value in the systematic teaching of reading to children of nursery school age: they will learn in far less time and with far less trouble when they have reached the right degree of maturity. Reading is a tool for getting second-hand information from the printed word, whereas these early years are the time for first-hand experience.

Writing

Writing goes hand in hand with reading, and you may be called upon to provide copies for notices saying such things as 'Road Works', 'No Entry', 'Private', etc. You will also write names on paintings, and sometimes titles or even stories. Do not over-emphasise the reading, but just say, 'There, that says 'Lucy' and that says 'Twins in high heels'. The children's use of pencils, felt-tip pens, etc. is all good practice for learning to write. They should not be expected to do 'writing patterns', though some of the older ones may enjoy learning to write their names. Some children are taught to write at home, usually in capitals, and it is then helpful if you can offer the parents the print-script forms that are used at the school to which the child will go at five. This is also a good opportunity to urge that neither reading nor writing should be forced on the child, but that he should be allowed to come to them in his own good time.

Pre-maths Opportunities

These are so much a part of the nursery school experience that they are not always recognised as such. We count, of course—milk-bottles, children, chairs, and we use rhymes about number, but think also of the mathematical experience involved in shopping, weighing cookery ingredients, measuring the tallest child, building with bricks, checking the temperature, and so on. What about time—by the clock and by the calendar? What about the different sizes and shapes of painting paper? What about the changing shape of a lump of clay that is pounded, rolled, cut, grated? What about water-play? Sand play? The children do not need to match figure 2 with two dots and figure 8 with eight dots; they need plenty of experience with twos and eights, and many and few, with long and short, and heavy and light, with full and empty, and high and low, so as to gain an understanding on which later number work can be accurately based.

In these days a great deal of emphasis is laid on never missing the 'teaching moment'. This *is* important, and requires you to be alert so that you recognise the child's readiness for further information and his openness to your attempts to supply it. This may be done by talking and discussion, by demonstration (very seldom!), by producing an apt illustration or a relevant book. If you find, by the lack of response, that you have misjudged the moment, then let the matter drop.

The satisfying of the child's intellectual needs is not in any way separate from the provision you make for his creative or his emotional development, the various aspects of his personality being interdependent. Always remember that you are dealing with the whole child.

13

Spiritual Growth

Everything the child experiences either helps or hinders his spiritual development. It is our humanity we share with others of whatever language, race or class; it is only as far as we are fully human that we can develop spiritually. If, at home, the child is loved and accepted as part of the family; if at school he is welcomed and valued as part of the group; if, in turn, he is helped to love, welcome and accept others, then his life is gaining a true spiritual dimension. If, on the other hand, he hears talk disparaging others, if he sees a child rejected, an 'outsider' ignored, then his spiritual growth is retarded. This remains true whether or not he is taught to say his prayers at home, to join in a 'morning ring' at nursery school, or is sent to Sunday school. So what can we do?

Firstly we can teach him the value of human personality by our welcoming manner towards him and towards everyone else at school. (There is no need to be effusive, indeed, over-effusiveness is apt to sound hypocritical, when just a smile and a word will express your pleasure.) Next we must teach him that we are all 'members one of another', that 'no man is an island', that being human involves living in society. If you exclude a tiresome child from the group, if you sit him in miserable isolation for some misdemeanour, if you turn your back on him when he has been unkind or aggressive then you are teaching him that only the good are acceptable. Society has to learn to carry its weaker members, and this learning should begin in pre-school days.

Still considering this most important area of personal relationships, you must awaken his sensitivity to, his sympathy for the needs and sadnesses of others. You may do this by your sympathetic handling of a distressed child, and by suggesting something that the individual or the group could do to make him happy: maybe something as simple as 'Let's sing "Oats and beans and barley grow" because Dan likes it and it will cheer him up'. You may do it by your choice of story, when your group's sympathy is aroused for 'The Outside Cat', or for poor shivering Jacko on his journey from Africa to snowy Scotland.

This 'reverence for life' (to use Albert Schweitzer's phrase) you should extend to living creatures and to plants. Teach your children to *look*, to *see*: in this way they will be led to wonder, and so to reverence. The child who has really *seen* a spider, who has looked at its many legs, its scuttling movements, its beautiful web, will not carelessly crush one. The child who has helped to care lovingly and tenderly for the school rabbits and guinea-pigs will show this care for animals in later life. The child who has watched the germinating seeds and growing plants will not destroy the trees and plants in the park. The growth of six or eight feet of sunflower plant from a small seed is miraculous whether you believe it happens because of God's ordering or as the result of natural forces. Four-year-old Mary, on hearing in a hymn 'God made the sun, and God made me' retorted, 'God didn't make me—I grew in Mummy's tummy'. It might be said that both statements were valid, with the individual's point of view deciding which was acceptable, but it seems to me that both can be true as they are different ways of saying the same thing. The beauty of the environment that you prepare for them, the laughter and the love that you share with them, these will speak to your children of the spiritual reality that some call humanity and some call God.

So does it matter whether you teach your under-fives to sing hymns, to say prayers, to listen to Bible stories? Yes, I think it does . . . It is virtually impossible to avoid giving children of this age false ideas derived from misunderstood hymns (four-year-old Carole always sang 'For little Jesus' steak' instead of 'sake') and from inaccurately repeated prayers. You can insist that all put their hands together, that all close their eyes, but you have no control over their thoughts, you have no idea what concepts of God they are forming. The say-after-me-type of prayer means nothing to most of the children, whilst the learned-by-heart prayer is usually repeated mechanically. If something especially happy has happened, how much better to say 'Let's all be quite quiet a moment, and think how lovely it has been to watch the snow and play in it'. If someone is ill, why not suggest, 'Let's all be very quiet a minute, and think about poor So-and-So, and about the doctors and nurses who are trying to make him better, and about his Mummy who is sad because he is ill'. Grace before meals is better when it becomes thanks (to Cook?) after meals. After all, what does 'Thank you for the world so sweet' mean to a young child? Tossy (his own version of Thomas) always sang at home 'Thank you for the worms so sweet'. Can you think of a hymn that is really intelligible to a child of this age from a non-church background—and remember that most children are from such a background? And then take Bible stories—what can you safely tell? 'The Lost Sheep', 'The Good Samaritan' perhaps. None of the miracles, almost nothing from the old Testament—Moses in the bullrushes is too frightening with its wholesale slaughter of babies, whilst I have not told 'Noah's Ark' since a shocked child asked me 'But what happened to all the others?'

And Christmas? All our babies are special to their families, and we rejoice together in nursery school when a new baby comes. At Christmas we talk about just one special baby who was called Jesus, and we tell the stories and sing the carols that everyone knows, that are a part of our national heritage. Christmas is a time for giving, not only for getting: one of the most religious stories I know does not once mention God or Jesus. It is 'Matthew and Eva in the Toyshop' and is all about the efforts of two children to buy each other a secret present. Let us enjoy Christmas together, making decorations, making presents to take home, singing carols, preparing for the party, and omitting everything that leads to tension, strain, overtiredness. 'God rest you merry'.

You may accuse me of secularism, or atheism. Not so. I am anxious that these children should have their spiritual development so nurtured that their growing sensitivity and awareness are not damaged by the too-early presentation of religious ideas. It is the truth of the spiritual dimension of life that you should show them. 'Let your lives speak'.

14

Language with the Less Voluble

It is not possible in one short section to do more than make a few points relevant to any work you might undertake in 'language expansion' with children of poor linguistic ability, but I must emphasise that all work done with these children should be related to current interests and activities in the school, and must be part of its daily life. Language *is* part of daily life.

The imported 'language kits' are designed to teach the appropriate verbal response to a stimulus, which is usually visual: e.g. 'What is this?' 'It is an apple'. 'What colour is it?' 'It is red'. This is easy (though dull) for the teacher, who only has to follow the instructions, and easy for the child, who only has to form the habit of making the right response. Is this valuable? Perhaps it is—but it does not fulfil what is, in my opinion, the aim of any 'language enrichment' work done in the nursery school. I believe that the children should be helped to develop lively, spontaneous language that is useful in their everyday life and adequate for their later more formal learning. It should be your aim to make them *want* to talk, to give them first-hand experiences to talk about, and to introduce into their language essential grammar and vocabulary, along with the fluency and rhythm of good speech.

Most children want to communicate, at however primitive a level. Encourage this by talking to the child as an individual: on his arrival greet him by name, comment on a new tie or a cut finger, tell him how much you missed him when he was absent. Make him feel a valued person, show him you are glad to listen to him, encourage him to show you his treasures and his work, to share with you his joys and his sorrows. However busy you are, it really takes no longer to say, 'I do like that bright red patch in your painting' than it does to say 'Very nice, dear'. A smiling 'Just a minute, and then I'll have a good look' will encourage him to stay by you until you have finished your immediate job and are free to discuss his work with him. Develop a sensitivity to the needs of those children you just cannot afford to dismiss with a bare comment, those who have little experience of being listened to, of being valued for themselves. These children must always be included in the conversation, must be drawn to you with one arm whilst you are busy with another child; their tentative approaches must never be ignored. In the hurly-burly of free play for all, make sure that whilst every child receives some attention, the most needy get most.

Whilst you are working in this way to make the children eager to communicate, you must also work to give them something worth talking about. They need the vividness of first-hand experience: not, for instance, the cold sterility of a plastic fruit, but the sticky reality of a juicy orange that they have been to the shops to buy. Children from restricted home backgrounds need those experiences which are of the stuff of everyday life—making tea, sweeping, washing-up, polishing furniture, cooking, etc., and they need an adult to talk to them about the work in hand, and to recall it afterwards. They need what has been aptly described as 'mental companionship', they need someone to listen when they talk, and to reply. Arrange to repeat the experience, perhaps several times, and encourage the children to talk about it and to recall what they did. Use any suitable voluntary helpers that you can get. Ask your head teacher's permission to take small groups of children to explore the environment: visit the park to pick up leaves or to feed the ducks, visit the supermarket to buy the ingredients for cookery, visit the fire station, the police station, the river, the canal. Even if you are not able to take the children out of school, you can still make good use of the play environment. Create a replica in miniature of the district, with cartons or wooden blocks painted to resemble the shops in the High Street, with toy cars to push along a painted road, a green-painted park, a painted nursery school, and clothes peg or cotton reel people to represent the children and their families. Supply some simple dolls' house furniture and some pipe-cleaner dolls to play with and to talk about. Stimulate *all* their senses, touch, taste and smell as well as sight and hearing. Let them *feel* their bodies—stretch, stride, twist, turn, balance, rock.

The children will learn rhythms of speech from hearing you talk, from listening to well-told stories, from joining in finger-play rhymes. Apart from speech rhythms, the children need to be helped to enlarge their vocabulary, but it is always experience that is of the first importance: the words to describe the experience must follow, not precede it. I once heard someone trying to teach the words 'transparent' and 'opaque' by showing the group a plastic bag (which was translucent, not transparent!) and a paper bag: she was not able to understand that the children needed lots of experience with materials that were opaque and materials that were transparent *before* she tried to teach the words. On the other hand, do make full verbal use of any experience or activity: e.g. the ball that you kick is not only round, it is also hard (or soft), plain (or patterned), red or blue or multi-coloured. You kick it hard—or gently, high—or low, a long way—or a short distance. You can play observation games— 'What can you see that is red and soft and woolly and cosy?' 'Who is wearing black shoes and long socks and a blue dress with pink buttons and a pink hair ribbon?' You can make up jingles, to such tunes as 'The Mulberry Bush':

'Mary is wearing a new red dress, new red dress, new red dress,
Mary is wearing a new red dress this bright and sunny morning'.

Use your ingenuity to make language alive, interesting, expressive, to make it FUN.

Then think of grammar: does the child use plurals, or is it always 'two dog', 'lots of apple'? What about verbs?—he probably uses the present tense, and also a possibly inaccurate past tense:' buyed', 'catched', 'runned'—all wrong but all showing that he has an idea of how to form a past tense. Adverbs seem to come fairly easily: 'Carry it carefully', 'Run quickly', etc., though it is common for the final—'ly' to be omitted. Prepositions often give trouble: 'It's under the table', is quite easy; 'It's under that book'—not so easy; 'Crawl under the table'—much more difficult. Then pronouns: 'he' and 'she', 'him' and 'her' may be confused: and possessives—'mine' is easy and 'yourn' is logical, even though inaccurate; 'his' and 'hers' come fairly easily, but 'theirs' is difficult. To go back to verbs: imperatives seem to come naturally—'Put my coat on', but you will probably have to teach 'Would you put my coat on?'; 'may' and 'can' are confused by many adults as well as children; the passive tense may be understood, but is hardly ever used; e.g. 'Peter knocked my bricks down' rather than 'My bricks were knocked down by Peter'. Be aware of these points in your own speech and vary it accordingly. Listen to the child's speech, and notice whether he is missing out plurals, or adjectives, or whatever, so that you can make a point of including these in your talk with him.

Throughout all this work, it is, however, important to remember that fluency is more important than accuracy, and that it is more helpful to expand what the child has said than to correct it. For example: 'Daddy gorn a work'. 'Yes, your Daddy has gone to work, and he will come home this evening. What will you do when you see him?' In this way, you have *a* unobtrusively corrected his error; *b* added a new dimension to his statement; *c* asked a question, to encourage him to continue the conversation. There is a sensitivity, an openness, even a skill which can be learned with practice, in encouraging a child to talk and in developing his use of lanauage. It is possible to feel towards the topic that will draw an individual into conversation, whether it be boats, or Dougal, or fish and chips, or policemen . . . The large group situation may inhibit any attempt to talk, but to be part of a small group may well help a child more than to have you talk to him alone. In short, sensitise yourself to the role of language, to a certain extent programme *yourself*, but keep your work with the children free, 'ad hoc', arising from current interests and activities.

When assessing the child's language you will probably find it helpful to use a simple check list; there is one at the end of this section. A quick and easy way of using this is to cut a number of sheets of tracing paper to a suitable size, and then punch holes at the top to take loose-leaf rings or tags; you will need three sheets per child. Copy the headings 'Name', 'Address', etc. on a smooth card the same size as the tracing paper, and copy the check lists on to the left-hand side of cards about 8 cm wider than the tracing paper. Rule several columns on the remainder of the card. Slip the first card under the first sheet of tracing paper and fill in particulars about the child in the right places, then remove the card. Slip the first wide card under the second sheet, leaving the questions legible on the left-hand side. Tick as appropriate, leaving the spaces blank rather than putting a cross, and then repeat with the other card under the third sheet. You will be able to 'read off' very easily any individual's present state and his progress, if any, by replacing the appropriate card under the tracing paper. Children with language difficulties should be checked at least every month, others less frequently. You may want to add check lists for social development, types of play, etc. These could conveniently be in the same form, and be filed with the child's language assessment papers.

Special help with language enrichment can be given to small groups through such activities as the following:

1 Brick play, including traffic toys. This play gives practice especially with prepositions; e.g. under, on top, beside, through.
2 Dolls' house play, leading to talk about family relationships and activities.
3 Cooking and cleaning, especially those activities likely to be seen at home, such as making tea and washing-up, so that language is attached to home activities as well as school.
4 Shopping, with a list made beforehand with the children's help, and the items then selected by the children, paid for by them, the change taken, and the shopping carried back to school.
5 'Neighbourhood play', with simple models of streets, shops, and other buildings.
6 Scrapbooks, using pictures brought by the *children* (this is important) even if only news cuttings.
7 Finger-play rhymes and singing games adapted for particular language needs: e.g. to the tune 'Twinkle, twinkle little star'
       'Put your hands high in the air,
       Put your hands low on the ground'

8 Simple stories, especially those clearly illustrated with a series of pictures; e.g. 'Topsy and Tim' stories.

Whatever special work you undertake, use your intelligence and your zest for life to stir the children from unseeing apathy, to draw them from heedless boisterousness, to free them from restricted lives, to help them to live.

Check List for assessment of language, and rough diagnosis of areas requiring special help

FIRST CARD: CHILD'S PARTICULARS

Name	Date of birth
Address	Date of admission
Father's occupation	
Mother's occupation	
Position in family	
Home language background	
Special help to be given	

SECOND CARD

1 *a* Talks/babbles to self while playing					
b Talks freely to children					
familiar adults					
d all adults					
2 Explains/describes *a* clearly and vividly					
b using phrases/gestures as substitutes					
c inadequately					
3 Understands questions *a* present					
b past					
c hypothetical					
4 Answers questions fully					
inadequately					
5 Answers either/or questions					
6 Asks questions— where?					
who?					
when?					
how?					
why?					
7 Instructions: carries out accurately					
approximately					
disregards					
8 Uses book corner with interest					
superficially					
9 Storytime: listens with interest					
understands plot					
joins in rhymes/finger-play					

THIRD CARD

10 Pronunciation: *a* good					
b adequate					
c needs treatment					
11 Sentences: one-word					
phrases					
complex					
Use of grammar					
nouns					
plural nouns					
verbs— present tense					
past					
future					
conditional					
passive					
adverbs					
adjectives					
pronouns					
possessives					
prepositions					
comparatives					

Notes on interpretation of check list questions

1 Failure in *b* or *c* suggests shyness rather than language poverty.

2 *a* and *b* overlap as few children talk without some gesture: record as *b* gesture used in place of speech.

3 e.g. *a* 'Is that a new pair of shoes?'
    b 'Did Mummy buy you those shoes?'
    c 'Will Mummy buy you some new shoes when those wear out?'

5 'Would you like a chocolate, or a sweet?' 'Yes' is not an acceptable answer.

7 e.g. 'Please will you put this book away on the bottom shelf of the book rack?' Putting it on table or wrong shelf is 'approx'
    Taking it but not putting it away is 'disregards'

8 'Interest' is following story from pictures,
    looking carefully at illustrations
    discussing book with adult or child, etc., etc.
'Superficially' is turning pages inattentively
    merely glancing at book, etc., etc.

10 *b* includes immature pronunciations that will probably disappear as child matures.

 c means requiring help of speech therapist.

15

The Teacher's Role

An earlier chapter dealt with various aspects of the child's adjustment to life in the nursery school group; this deals with your role as teacher. Try always to be welcoming and understanding, and never totally reject an individual, even though his behaviour be unacceptable: this is essential, and, though sometimes difficult, is never impossible!

At the Start of the Session

The children should come into school not all at the same time, but over a period of some fifteen to twenty minutes, so that you can greet them individually by name, comment on new shoes or a special toy, and gratefully receive presents, which may be anything from a tattered drawing to a child-made gingerbread man, or from a dusty bunch of ragwort to a shoulder-bag containing a varied assortment of worms, spiders and slugs 'for the nature table'. You must also be available to greet parents, together with visiting aunts and grandpas, and to listen to any item of interest or concern about the children. Mothers should feel free to stay a while to watch their children playing or to look at interesting things in the room; this gives you an opportunity quietly to comment to the parent on progress in the child's play, and also to encourage interest in what the school is trying to do, perhaps enlisting the parents' help.

The child who finds it difficult to say goodbye to his mother may be helped by being taken to the window 'to wave goodbye', or by being involved in some activity with an adult. Some children bring personal possessions to school and may like to put them safely in the 'treasure box' after showing them to their friends, whilst others will want to hold them, keeping a precious link between home and school. Some children need 'to stand and stare', or to stay beside you, until they are ready to become involved, and should not be hurried into activity. The child who has been under tension before coming to school may need some help to settle down to work; a quiet word from you, showing that you understand and regret the difficulty, will be helpful.

Rules and Guidelines

In any community some rules are necessary: in nursery school the rules should be few, clear, and observed. Some rules deal with safety matters, some teach children to use apparatus correctly, some are concerned with an individual's freedom of action. In addition to the few necessary rules, you will do well to build up a body of customs, conventions and traditions which help towards peace and happiness in the group, but which entail no great misfortune if they are not always observed. These include the common courtesies, such as not pushing, not snatching, not sitting on someone else's chair. Children can be helped to 'do as you would be done by', but should never be treated on the principle of 'be done by as you did'. At all times you must be in control, however unobtrusively, since full responsibility for his behaviour is too heavy a burden for the young child, but at the same time you must be on the child's side: 'Yes, I know you're cross, because you had a row with Mummy before you came to school, but all the same, I can't let you do that'. Whenever possible, find a substitute activity, or change the subject, or suggest a new idea: 'Come and see what I have in my cupboard', may lead to a chocolate drop or a new game.

PHYSICAL SAFETY

Depending on the premises and the apparatus available, a few common-sense rules are essential: e.g. you must not go out of the gate without an adult, you must not climb on the boundary fence, you must not threaten anyone with tools or scissors, you must not play with electrical apparatus or power points. When new children are admitted you must teach them these rules, but you must also arrange that supervision is effective: children should not be in a position to break safety rules deliberately, though they may do so forgetfully. You will find that a friendly, but firm, warning is usually sufficient, but it may be necessary quietly but firmly to use 'sanctions': e.g. 'You must play indoors for a little while, to remind you not to climb on the fence'; 'You can finish making your boat tomorrow when you can remember that hammers are only for banging nails'. Children should be given *one* warning—repeated warnings encourage them to see how far they can go—and should know what to expect if they disregard it. Do not continue the 'sanction' for too long, certainly not after the end of the session, and, although it may be helpful to remind the child on the following day, it will often be better to 'let bygones be bygones'.

KEEPING CONTROL OF THE GROUP

Rules and guidelines are necessary for the group, but your ability to control your group gently and sensitively needs something more. This control is sometimes difficult for students on teaching practice, but as it is largely a question of the relationship between children and teacher, it proves easier when they have finished training and have their own group. Nevertheless, for those who do find it a problem, a solution will include the following points:

a Remember first of all that control is essential—without it, children feel insecure, play deteriorates, equipment gets lost or broken. It is better to begin by being very firm, and then easing off when you have the situation well in hand.

b Provide enough for every child to be busy; the child totally involved in a play activity does not indulge in antisocial behaviour.

c Take an interest in *all* that is going on in the playroom, rather than devoting all your attention to one activity.

d Make sure the children know what behaviour is acceptable and what is inappropriate: e.g. at the water tray, experiments with fountains may be messy, but are permissible, whereas deliberately throwing water on the floor is not. Be consistent, and do not sometimes permit behaviour which you condemn on other occasions.

e Beware of giving more attention to bad than to good behaviour: some children may never have learned that being good is noteworthy.

f Keep your voice quiet and your manner calm. If you try to shout above the noise, the children will copy you; a quiet positive request to a child is more effective—not 'Stop shouting', but 'Will you use a quieter voice, please'.

Clearing-up

The clearing-up period inevitably entails some confusion. The children can be expected to clear up their own activities, but they will need encouragement and, possibly, some help. Distinguish between jobs that must be completed at the time, such as clearing and cleaning the creative table, and those that can well be done at the end of the session, such as checking constructional toys. Children respond to a reasonable request, such as 'If you can't find a job to do, would you get your story chair and sit quietly until we are all ready.' When you begin clearing the room, it is sensible to pack up first any activities not in current use, whilst warning the children to finish what they are doing, as it is nearly clearing-up time. If every activity is in use then after due warning, clear up the messiest first, enlisting the help of the children who have been working there.

When the room is adequately tidied and the group is together in the story ring, an action song or finger-play rhyme will catch everyone's attention, thus quietening any noisy children and enabling you to start the story. Any child who does not want to listen should be free to move elsewhere.

At the End of the Session

Homegoing should be spread over a period in the same way as arrival; at hometime it may well be helpful to rule that all children play *in the room* until called for. You must see that there are enough interesting things for all to do, even if the messier activities like clay and paint have been cleared away, as there should never be a time when children have nothing to do but wait: this is a waste of their time, and does not make a happy end to the day. When parents come for their children, comment on any praiseworthy activity of their child, but not on any misdemeanour, and say a friendly goodbye. Children should have the opportunity to take home their work if they want to, and should have their personal treasures returned to them. (It must be explained to new children that this *is* the return of personal property, and not the giving of gifts to a chosen few.) You must, of course, report any accident, and also explain if a child has been changed into school clothes.

It will sometimes happen that a child is left after all the others have gone home. You must be sensitive to any sign of tension or distress, and try to give a reasonable explanation for the delay, such as 'I expect your Mum's clock has stopped', or 'Perhaps your Mummy is still waiting at the bus stop', or whatever is appropriate in the circumstances. The child may be willing to help you 'get ready for the afternoon children', or to 'make a lovely picture to give Mummy when she comes', but you must assure him *a* that he *will* be called for, and *b* that you will look after him until someone comes. When a child first joins the group, try to arrange with the parents that he is amongst the first to be called for, at any rate for a few days, until he is secure in the knowledge that everyone goes home at the end of the session. If a mother knows that she will be late calling for her child, because of a hospital appointment or some such reason, she should explain this to him, and also tell you, so that you can remind him just before hometime.

16

Supervision

Soon after I started teaching, an H.M.I. told me that I ought to know what each one of my children was doing every minute of the day! I still think, as I did then, that this was an impossible task, but there is a basic soundness in the injunction. As teachers, we are responsible for what the children in our groups are doing; we are responsible for their physical safety, and for the ways in which they use their time at school. It would, however, be a serious mistake to think that supervision is all that is necessary, for nursery school teaching is far more than just 'giving an eye' to what they are doing. I am not going to elaborate this here, because the whole book is about involvement, and the role of the teacher is implicit in all I have written. I do want to remind you, though, that although you may be involved with one group of children, you are still responsible for all the others. If you are in the playground, move amongst them and join in their play. Although you must see that the climbing apparatus and the slide are used safely, this does not mean that you must remain rooted to the spot! It would be foolish—and foolhardy—to sit reading to a child if you were the only adult in the garden, but you can safely be a passenger in a train, a prisoner in a jail, or a mummy in a garden house while you are keeping an eye on the other play that is going on. You will need to watch that the bigger children are careful when playing with the wheeled toys, so that the smaller ones are not knocked down. You should also see that they take 'turns eaches', as some of my children say, with the more popular equipment. It is not sufficient to 'supervise' the garden through the playroom window; not only would you be unable to forestall an accident or to deal quickly with the result of one but you would also be unable either to show interest in the children's play, or to suggest ways in which it might be expanded.

You are also responsible for supervision indoors. Whatever you are doing, you must also watch that children playing with the water are wearing aprons and have their sleeves rolled up properly, that those at the sand are not throwing it, that those in the music corner are not misusing the instruments. You must remember those children whose bladder control is weak, and who need to be reminded to go to the lavatory, but who may not be able to manage alone. If a child needs to wash his hands, you must see that his sleeves are rolled up and that he is properly dry when he has finished: it is not enough just to tell him to go and wash unless you are sure he is competent. Be aware of potentially dangerous items: scissors, which should be used only at the creative and sewing tables, and not be carried around the room; glass bottles, which are not suitable for shop or water play; steel knives which must not be available for the children's play, but which may be used under supervision for cookery or at meal-times; even a pointed pencil may inflict a nasty wound if used as a weapon. If the children are allowed to play in other rooms, such as the office or staff-room, remember to keep an ear on their activities, and to visit them sometimes: they should not be allowed to play in any room where there is danger from a cooker, a washing machine, a hot iron, etc. In all rooms, make sure there is no danger of burning from an electric heater, or from a power point.

Supervision of Staff

Arrange with your assistant that if you are in the garden she is responsible inside, and vice-versa, and make sure she realises how much she can contribute to the children's play. She will probably have some domestic chores for which she is responsible: see that she has time to attend to these satisfactorily; encourage her to let the children help with these jobs.

If you have a nursery student, she can share the chores, but they should not all be loaded on to her, as not only should she learn through her practical work with the children, she should also have an opportunity to enjoy the play activities. You are responsible for seeing that she learns about all aspects of the work of a nursery assistant; she should sometimes join your storytelling and music groups and, later on should, under supervision, tell a story to a small group, and enjoy some musical activities with them. You may be asked by her tutor to fill in a report form on her work, etc., and this you must do with great care, remembering that not only does the girl's future depend on her training, but also that of all the children she may work with after her training is finished. If you have a new student whose ability you seriously doubt, discuss this with your head teacher, for it might be better if the girl were encouraged to consider taking up a different career.

17

Working with Other Adults

The 'atmosphere' in your group will depend not only on your relationship with the children, but also on your attitude to the different adults with whom you have contact during school hours. It is most important that the children should learn from you to treat people in a friendly and courteous way, to see them as individuals each with his own work to do, his own life to lead. Whilst visitors need not make an approach to the children, they must respond to a smile, a question, a request; they may make a negative response; 'I'm sorry, I must just do this writing', but it must be a person-to-person communication.

One of your most important relationships is with your head teacher; I feel it would be impertinent for me to offer advice on this, so I shall not add anything to my remarks in the Preface.

The Nursery Assistant

A very great deal of help with your work in school will be given by your nursery assistant, and although she will not have had the privilege of teacher-training as you have, yet she may have had many years' experience. It is not easy for a mature woman or a trained and experienced nursery nurse to feel that she has to work 'under' an inexperienced teacher, and indeed she should not have to, because the emphasis should be on your working *together*. She knows the children in your group, and may have known their families over a period of years and so, although she may have no theoretical knowledge of their difficulties, she will probably have a practical understanding of their behaviour, together with a real relationship with them and their parents. When you first 'take over' a group you must

I

accept that the children will turn more naturally to their familiar friend, your nursery assistant, than to you, and you must be prepared gradually to build up a relationship with them.

This said, you still have to determine *your* role as teacher and *her* role as assistant, and you have to bear in mind that it is the way *you* regard the work with the children that will influence her for good or ill. I have always made it a rule never to ask my assistant to do anything that I was not prepared to do, on occasion, myself. For instance, it is generally the case that you, as teacher, are more often busy with the children, whereas the assistant may more often be busy with the chores, but if she is involved with a group of children, and you find the bathroom floor needs wiping, then you will do it —and while you are doing it, you will talk to the children who have followed you in about dry and wet floorcloths, about where the clean water comes from and where the dirty water goes. Again, your assistant may well wash paintpots while you are telling a story, but that is no reason for exploiting her: if there has been a very messy period of creativity, offer to help her after the children have gone home, rather than leaving her to face a daunting pile in the sink. With regard to the children's toilet-training, in my school we have an unwritten agreement that whoever finds a child with dirty pants, washes and changes him, but on the other hand, if I am very busy, I may say to my assistant, 'Jimmy's dirty: could you cope, please?' and I remember to thank her afterwards.

While the children are at school you will, on the whole, be too busy to find time to chat, but there are times when it is helpful to comment on a child's behaviour—out of his hearing. It may just be, 'Did you notice? Linda went to the bathroom by herself', or perhaps, 'Look how Luke and Robert are working together'. After the children have gone home, you can talk it over together and plan ways of further boosting Linda's confidence, or of promoting co-operation between Robert and Luke. Try always to work out together a consistent way of dealing with child behaviour; if your assistant does not agree with you, ask her to try it for a few days your way, and then talk about it again. She may have been right, when you can acknowledge it, and give in gracefully. You may have been right, when you can say, 'Our plan seems to be working, doesn't it?' One more point: you will try to have a reasonably permissive régime in the group, but make sure it is not so over-permissive that your assistant is obliged to be authoritarian in an attempt to keep order!

THE ASSISTANT'S ROLE IN THE DAILY PROGRAMME

Like the teacher, the nursery assistant should be in school half an hour before the children arrive. A cup of tea makes a welcome start to the day and can be drunk while she helps to get the room ready, to mix the paint, to cut up the paper, tidy the cupboards and so on. When the children arrive she should be free to work with them, and, if you are busy with a parent, should be alert to deal with any untoward incident. She will see that the children have what they need for their chosen activity, and that they put on aprons when necessary. During the session, if some children are playing out-of-doors your assistant will be with them while you are indoors, and vice-versa. At story and music times she will be with those children who have chosen not to take part, but you should arrange that she comes to these groups whenever possible: in this way she will learn to deal in acceptable ways with these two periods, and will become better equipped to undertake them if for any reason you are unable to.

When you are planning your day's programme, make a point of working out what you want your assistant to do, as well as what to do yourself: i.e. when you are busy at the clay, and are also supervising the painting and the water-play, ask her to be interested in the brick play while keeping an eye on the home corner and the puzzle table. It will be her job to prepare and serve the children's milk, etc., with their help, and to clear it away at the end. She should sometimes be invited to initiate and carry through a group activity, such as making jam tarts or polishing the furniture, and during this time *you* will be responsible for milk, bathroom, etc. When you ask her to undertake some such activity, mention any points you want her to emphasise, such as weighing ingredients, washing hands, care of furniture, etc.

When it is time to get ready for the mid-day meal, your assistant will take the children to wash their hands, help them with their meal, supervise the pre-rest toilet routine, and see that the bathroom is left clean and tidy. She should also make sure that it is in reasonable condition during the play periods and that any spills are dealt with by the children concerned, though with her help, if necessary. She should also keep the spare-clothes-cupboard tidy, seeing that the garments are clean, sorted, and neatly folded so that they are ready for use.

The main cleaning of the room will be done by the school cleaner, but your assistant will be responsible for some things, and can normally do them with the help of the children. These include keeping the home corner furniture and covers clean and attractive, occasionally scrubbing the building bricks, and wiping with a damp cloth the lorries, etc., in the brick corner, seeing that the dressing-up clothes are clean and mended, with loops for hanging, cleaning and tidying cupboards, and, in full-day schools, helping the children set out and put away the rest beds, and also scrubbing combs and boiling flannels, where these are still used. All this, together with other jobs not listed, add up to a fair amount of not very interesting 'chores', so do make sure that she has some interesting satisfying work as well.

I would like to stress that whatever your assistant undertakes, the overall responsibility is yours; you should exercise this responsibility not by 'inspecting' the work done, but by showing interest and appreciation, and by making sure her work is not increased by your thoughtlessness.

The Kitchen Staff

Nursery school children are no longer expected to sing (or say) grace before their mid-day meal—it is recognised that they cannot feel 'truly grateful' to an invisible God—but they *can* run into the kitchen and thank Cook for a dinner they have enjoyed. If the premises are suitable and Cook is willing, they can watch the preparation of the meal, but must not be allowed to hinder the kitchen staff, or to risk accidents with hot pans or ovens. You should talk to the children about cooking, about Cook and her helpers, about how pleased she is when everything is eaten. These days it is not usually the nursery school teacher's job to plan the meals, this being done by the cook or an employee of the School Meals Service, but Cook will be glad to hear from you if anything has been particularly enjoyed, and will also appreciate an explanation if you have had to send back any quantity of food. When the children do cooking, encourage them to save some for the kitchen staff, and to take it in to them themselves.

Domestic Staff

Whether you actually meet the cleaner or not, be careful not to give her extra work by allowing the children to be careless with the play material. If you feel you have any cause for complaint about the cleanliness of the room, mention it to your head teacher. Your cleaner will feel valued as a person if you sometimes leave her, with a little note, a bun that the children have cooked or a picture they have painted. In the same way you can make some personal recognition of the laundrywoman's contribution.

The caretaker or schoolkeeper will probably enjoy talking with the children and, men being in short supply in most nursery schools, he will be welcomed by them, especially if he will let them 'help' repair broken toys, etc.

Medical Staff

The school nursing sister will probably visit your children once a week; encourage them to look on her as a friend, to talk to her about their activities, and to show her their bumps and cuts. On her weekly visit you should bring to her notice any child you have seen scratching his head unduly, as well as any rash, septic condition or persistent sore. Once a term she will probably inspect their heads for cleanliness, and you can explain the day before what she will do. If you should find that you have caught headlice yourself, there is no need to panic: wash your hair at once with a special shampoo obtainable from the chemist, or perhaps from the school nurse, and all will be well! Head infestation is much less common than it used to be, but it is as well to be alert to the possibility.

When a medical inspection is due, make a point of discussing it with the whole group. Some children have a very real fear of the doctor, perhaps because of a time in hospital away from mother, or because of painful treatments or injections, and you should do anything you can to help them overcome this fear. Tell them when the doctor is coming, what her name is, that she is a friend of yours, that she is coming 'to see how big and strong you are'. Describe what she will do and why and, if not all the children are to be seen, promise the 'unlucky' ones a turn next time. Any extremely nervous child can be assured that the doctor 'is only going to look', and that his mother will be there with him. It also helps to show him the room where the medical will take place, and the room where he will get undressed *and dressed*, and the tin from which he will get a Smartie after he has been seen: never make this conditional on his 'being good', because not all children find this possible under the circumstances, and it is bad enough to be swept by blind unreasoning fears without being further penalised. It is usually possible for a child to watch while his friend is examined, so that he knows exactly what to expect, but do be sure that his friend will not make a fuss! Having said all this, do not overdo the preparation; describe it as a normal event, and appear to take it for granted that the children will co-operate.

Students and Other Visitors

When you have visitors, welcome them into your room, but do not 'lay on' special activities because, unless for some reason they have asked to see some particular work, they should see the group as it is under normal conditions. Visitors will probably have been briefed by your head teacher, and there will be no need for you to do more than answer their questions, and perhaps, explain what you are doing. College of Education students will probably have been given a list of points to observe, and should have been instructed about being friendly without interfering, but you may have tactfully to discourage men students from over-stimulating boisterous play! If the students have observations to make, try not to let the children pester them for stories, etc., but encourage a friendly approach from both sides.

Students who come on teaching practice should be allowed to take over the group gradually, so that the children do not feel abandoned by you, their own teacher, and near the end of the practice, the student should warn them that she will be returning to college and will miss them all, but that you will be glad to be with them again. Even during final teaching practice, do not lose all contact with your group; try to welcome them on arrival, perhaps be around at home time, and tell them where you will be and what you will be doing when you are not in the room with them. Make them feel that the student has your support, and do all that you can to back her up, so that your group accepts her and welcomes the work she does with them.

18

Parents' Problems

However young and inexperienced you may feel, there will be occasions when a parent, usually a mother, turns to you for advice. At such a time, whilst not allowing your sense of inadequacy to get in the way of your attempt to help you must yet listen with humility and sensitivity to the problem brought to you. It is not always easy for a mother to admit that she is finding it difficult to deal with her child. (The mother who is unable to admit it is in even greater need of help, but this is a different problem.) Let us take one at a time the commoner problems with which you may be asked to help.

Feeding Problems

When double-session (half-day) nursery schools were first proposed by the (then) Ministry of Education, it was said by some that they would be unable to help with feeding problems. This, of course, is not so, because these are seldom problems about the child's intake of food, but about a faulty mother/child relationship that has grown up around the mealtime situation. The natural desire of a mother is to feed her baby: if for any reason the baby does not feed readily, a self-perpetuating situation of tension arises. This is usually put right by the advice of the doctor, midwife or health visitor, but in a few unfortunate cases it may persist for years, when every mealtime becomes a battle, resulting in both physical and mental ill-health for mother and child, and requiring expert help, possibly from the Child Guidance clinic, to right the situation. Fortunately you are unlikely to encounter so serious a problem, though if you suspect it you should report it to your head teacher so that she can bring it before the school doctor. Most feeding problems begin when the child is between one and two years old, though sometimes even earlier than this, when he realises that by refusing, or by just playing with his food, he can get his mother 'in a state'. This usually begins by chance, at that stage when a young child is so interested in the world around that he is literally too busy to eat. It is very difficult for a young mother to have her lovingly-prepared food rejected, and she is worried by the fear that her child will become undernourished, but a calm removal of the rejected food and an equally calm offer of appropriate food at the next mealtime will keep down the tension. The same treatment works with the child of nursery school age. He should not be expected to eat large servings, and neither should he be expected to eat foods that he dislikes intensely. A small attractively served helping of whatever is on the menu, with the opportunity to ask for a second helping, but with any uneaten food taken away and disposed of—*not* served up again later—and no snacks between meals, should be advocated. When you look at a bonny bouncing child whose mother complains, 'He doesn't eat a thing', you realise how unnecessary is mealtime fuss. If he eats cheese and eggs it does not matter if he does not touch meat. If he refuses bread and potatoes he will be spared the misery of being overweight. If he refuses green vegetables he may yet enjoy salads or fresh fruit. Reassure the mother that so long as her child is lively and well and is not losing weight, she need not worry about meals, but should just offer a good mixed diet, let him sometimes choose his menu, take him shopping, encourage him to help with the cooking, in fact, make food interesting, but not essential.

Sleeping Problems

Firstly, late bedtimes. 'You're very late again today, Mrs. X. Has anything gone wrong?' 'No, it's just that I can't get him up in the mornings'. 'I wonder why that is. Is he very late to bed?' 'Well, he won't go till we do and we do sit up a bit watching the telly'.

Well, what do you answer? It is easy enough to say that he ought to be in bed by 7.30 at the latest, and no nonsense about it, but perhaps Dad does not come in until late, and then he has his tea which he shares with the child, and then it is easier to let the child drowse in an armchair watching television than to have a scene when everyone is tired, put him screaming up to bed, and have him continually coming down to make certain he is not missing something interesting. So what do you say? A two-way approach is best, to mother and to child, and it may be better to start with the child. Talk with him about the need for sleep, about bedtimes, about going to bed like a good boy (children do, on the whole, *like* to be good, especially if it is made easy for them). Ask him to go to bed earlier so that he will grow big and strong. You can even offer him a little reward—a Smartie, a gold star, a picture for his scrapbook, in the morning if he went to bed a littler earlier than the night before. When he agrees to this bargain, say 'Now we'll tell Mummy and ask her to help.' If you back her up and she backs you up, the child, who wants to please you both, will gradually form better bed-time habits.

Secondly, difficulty in getting to sleep. This is a frequent problem in the long light summer evenings. 'Bed in Summer' from R. L. Stevenson's '*A Child's Garden of Verse*' reminds us that it is by no means a new problem:

> 'And does it not seem hard to you
> When all the sky is clear and blue
> And I should like so much to play
> To have to go to bed by day?'

It helps if the room can be darkened with thick curtains, so long as all air is not excluded, but it may be better to put bed-time a little later, and to allow the child to lie quietly looking at a book or playing with toys—glove puppets are ideal at this time—until he is able to drop off to sleep.

Some children, especially those of above average intelligence, find it difficult to get to sleep because they are thinking over the events of the day and planning what they will do on the morrow. If mother—or father—will talk quietly with the child while he is getting ready for bed, avoiding over-exciting romps, and then, when he is tucked up, read him a quiet bed-time story that has a

128

quiet peaceful ending—not a serial—give him a goodnight kiss, turn out the light, and leave the door slightly open so that he is not shut away from the continuing life of the home, this may well relax him enough to enable him to sleep.

A more serious cause of difficulty in getting to sleep is anxiety. Perhaps there is tension in the home, or at school, or the arrival of a new baby has made him doubt his secure place in his parents' affection. He will probably not be aware that he is troubled by this anxiety; he only knows that things are not as he would have them be. It is no use to *tell* such a child that of course you love him just as much, etc.; he needs the reassurance of many little demonstrations of love, he needs praise for his achievements, he needs a short time every day when he is 'the only one'. Our school doctor once replied to a mother who complained that her child was jealous of the baby; 'How would you feel if your husband brought home another woman, and said, "But of course I still love you just as much"?' At bed-time an extra hug, a story while cuddled up on Mummy's lap, a loving good-night, and the door left a little open, 'So that I can peep at you while you're asleep', all help to give the reassurance that he needs.

Thirdly come nightmares. These are so common among three- to four-year-olds that they can almost be considered as normal, but mothers often need advice on how to deal with them. Some children, when they wake, do not remember their dreams, but still suffer a very real terror. It helps a child to be woken right up and reassured that, 'It was only a nasty dream, and Mummy is with you, and it's all right now'. A drink of warm milk, a visit to the lavatory, a quiet tucking-up, and Mummy staying a few moments before turning out the light and returning to her own bed: this will probably be sufficient to settle him for the rest of the night. If, on the other hand, he remembers his dream, he will be helped by having the light put on and being encouraged to tell what is troubling him. Although it is 'only a dream' the terror is still very real to the child after he is awake. (I can still remember, after more than forty years, waking from a recurrent nightmare and lying rigid because, although my rational mind recognised it to be impossible, my whole being *knew* that spiders would run all over me if I moved even a tiny muscle). The child needs a little time awake to dispel this terror before he is encouraged to settle down once more. A child should never be laughed at for his night terrors, and should never be left to face them alone.

Lastly, the non-sleeping child. Some children need comparatively little sleep, and although 'non-sleeping' is a misnomer, it sometimes seems only too accurate to his suffering parents. Four-year-old Clive used to have sleeping tablets occasionally so that his mother could get some rest, as his normal sleep time was from 11 p.m. to 4 a.m. Such children should be under medical supervision, though it usually does them no harm to sleep for so short a period, and most family doctors would not regularly prescribe drugs. It may be possible for the parents to get some rest by doing 'night duty' turn and turn about, that is for one parent to 'sleep' in a single bed in the child's room, while the other has a good night's rest. Fortunately, such children usually grow out of this problem, but considerable endurance is demanded of their parents until they do.

Toilet Training

This so often becomes a problem, sometimes with several aspects. A young mother may feel it a reflection on herself if her child is not both clean and dry, particularly if she has a neighbour who tells her, 'I haven't had nappies on Susie since she was eleven months old'. The mother then gets tense, the tension is communicated to the child, and the situation worsens. If you can just reassure her that children gain control at different ages, that her child is perfectly normal, and that if she can be patient and loving, the imagined problem will be solved, then that is probably all that you need to do.

Occasionally, however, you come across a mother who, perhaps because of her own rigid upbringing, regards it as wicked that her child should have wet pants, and punishes him severely. I failed to help one such mother, who could not accept that her eldest son laughed, not to rile her, but because of embarrassment at his wet bed, whilst her child at nursery school was hindered, not helped to gain daytime bladder control by her severity and his grandmother's threats to put him 'in a deep dark hole'. We did the only thing we could to ease the problem for the boy; as soon as his mother left him at nursery school, we helped him to change into school trousers, explaining that then he would have dry trousers to go home and his mother would not be 'upset', and then, just before hometime we sent him to the lavatory and put on his own clothes again.

Parental attitudes apart, there are some children who *are* later gaining control, though this is not regarded by the special enuresis clinics as a problem requiring attention until the child is at least five years old. Dryness at night comes later than dryness during the day and, even when it has been achieved, it is easily lost again if the child is ill or upset. If the child has been dry but starts wetting again, he should be taken to the doctor in case there is a physical cause, such as an infection or a chill. Sometimes a change to colder weather will cause a lapse, and then warmer clothing or another blanket on the bed may help. The child needs to be reassured that he will soon be dry again, and that his mother knows that he cannot help it. Quiet, rather than lavish praise should be given when he is dry, whilst a quiet dealing with the wet bedding or pants is to be aimed at when he has a lapse—though it is not easy for a mother without adequate drying space to face with equanimity a series of wet sheets, particularly if she also has a baby's nappies to deal with. It sometimes helps if a child is 'lifted' when his parents go to bed, but if this is done, he must be woken up, because to allow him to pass water while he is still more or less asleep is to ask for trouble! If the lapse has an emotional cause, such as a hospital experience or the arrival of a new baby, reassurance and frequent demonstrations of continuing love are needed, as for the child who cannot sleep because of his anxiety. If a child has not achieved control yet, and if the doctor has checked that there is no physical cause, then really all the mother can do is to be patient! She can take him to the lavatory at reasonable intervals, she can put him in pants that are easy to manage, she can notice if he is wriggling or holding himself—usually an indication that he needs to go—but all this will be of little avail until he reaches the necessary maturity. Patience is all!

Sex Instruction

Some parents need to be reassured that it is both natural and normal for quite young children to want to know 'the facts of life', and they may need to be helped to deal with questions as they arise without embarrassment or prevarication. Two things are important: the child must be told nothing that is not true, and he should not be told more than he needs to know at that time. He will be both confused and bored if, when he just wants to know how the baby gets out of 'Mummy's tummy', he is given a long explanation of the whole process of human reproduction. Some parents prefer their children to learn that sex is a private matter, not to be discussed with all and sundry; some parents prefer not to be seen naked by their children; some parents find it perfectly reasonable that their children should share the bathroom and the lavatory with them. These are personal preferences that do not deserve either praise or blame. On the other hand, parents must realise that some children have a desire for privacy that must be respected. Jennifer's mother asked her teacher to explain to the child why she could not see her daddy undressed when he could see her in her bath. Jennifer had to learn that other people's feelings must be respected in this as in other matters, but Jennifer's father had to learn that his four-year-old daughter had sensibilities that *he* should respect.

Physical sex differences may be seen for the first time when children start at nursery school; they may be of great interest and some bewilderment, or they may go unnoticed, as in the story of the little girl from a protected background who went home from nursery school and told her mother that they had all been in the swimming pool. 'What, boys and girls together?' asked her shocked mother. 'Well, I don't really know,' replied the child. 'You see, they didn't have their clothes on'. Sex should be neither hidden nor over-stressed, but accepted as a normal part of life.

There is sometimes conflict with a parent who still believes that young children should be kept in ignorance of the facts of life. This may arise when a child takes home a drawing showing obvious sex differences, or when he shares in the ordinary nursery school talk about 'where babies come from'. You will then have to explain to the mother that it is better that children should be told facts, and that her child has been in no way harmed.

The Shy Child

Some children worry their mothers because they seem unduly shy, and will not answer when spoken to by neighbours or relatives, or willingly visit them or be 'minded' by them. It seems that the more an adult tries to make friendly contact, the more the child retreats. If you talk it over with the mother, you will often find that either she or her husband was like it as a child. You can reassure her that it is, if not absolutely normal, so common that she need not worry: after all, she (or he) grew out of it satisfactorily! If a child *is* painfully shy, it is much kinder to accept this and to limit the number of social occasions, whilst a few words on the quiet to grandparents or aunts to the effect that, 'He's going through a shy stage, so perhaps you would just say "hullo" and then leave it to him', may give the child the opportunity to respond when he feels able. One friend at a time to tea or to play for half an hour, one grown-up visitor, no being made to go out to tea—this is the way to help a child through this phase.

The Aggressive Child

This may be a more difficult problem to deal with for sometimes a child's mother or more often his father, is secretly proud of his ability to stick up for himself. In toddlers, aggression can be looked on as normal social contact, and you can explain that the young child with only a very limited command of language and no social graces is apt to approach his peers by kicking or hitting and is genuinely surprised when they cry! This stage soon passes if the child is shown more acceptable behaviour. A few older children are aggressive to get their own way, and parents should be advised not to allow them to enjoy their ill-gotten gains, but rather to insist that the coveted toy is returned with the assurance that his turn will come later when the other child has finished. On the other hand, children have to learn to fight their own battles, and no adult should intervene in such a way that a child comes to feel that he should never stand up for his rights. A child whose aggressiveness springs from a deep-seated hostility to life rather than from a straightforward desire to have what he wants when he wants it, needs skilled help, and some-one will have to undertake the delicate task of persuading his mother that it would be a measure, not of her inability to cope, but of her concern and caring, that she should seek skilled help from a Child Guidance Clinic. It is of the utmost importance that adults do not respond to aggression with further violence: though physical res-traint may be necessary, the child who hits should not be hit, the child who bites should not be bitten

Death

Death is a fact of life that has to be faced, and it is a mistake to try to shield a child from it, for he feels excluded. He must be allowed to share the grief, to talk about it, to cry about it, to come to terms with it, and he must be encouraged to remember the happiness shared with the one who has died. The fact of death can only be stated, not ex-plained. We none of us *know* what follows death, and I would think it better to withhold your own opinions and to allow his parents' explanation to stand, even if you do not agree with it. At school you can give him the opportunity to talk about it, and you should not discourage him from doing something that seems to you futile, but in which he finds an outlet for his love. Richard, a tough four-year-old, sat at the sewing table the day after his mother died and made 'a blue dress for my mummy to wear in heaven'. A bereaved child should not be overwhelmed with expressions of sympathy: he needs the opportunity to share in the grief, to have the comfort of a cuddle and to lead as normal a life as possible.

How do you explain burial? I wish I knew.

19

Keeping Your Head Above Water

If you are to be free to respond to the many demands made by the children and also to be sensitive to their unspoken needs, you will have to employ as many labour-saving devices as possible, so that your time and energy are not frittered away on non-essentials. And what are essentials? You must have reasonable priorities. Think what *is* important, what *really* matters. Spilled water, upset paint, are messy but not disastrous. A broken milk-bottle, a broken paste-jar must be quickly cleared away because of the danger from broken glass, but are not otherwise important. Comforting a distressed child comes before sweeping the floor. Following up the interest aroused by the discovery of an ant is more important than being 'on time' for a story. An uncommunicative child's attempt to talk to you should have priority over everything that is not 'a matter of life and death'. All through the day, try to be one jump ahead: forestall the temper tantrum by changing the subject quickly; have painting paper ready to hand; tie the water aprons securely; all the time try to save the time and trouble involved in putting things to rights by anticipating possible mishaps.

To take an obvious example: when a child is engrossed in his play, notice when he shows signs of needing to go to the lavatory, and then quietly remind him, promising to look after his game until he comes back. You will thus spare him the discomfort of wet pants, and yourself or your assistant the job of changing him, wiping up the floor, and rinsing out his wet clothes. A child who is not able to manage alone in the lavatory must be taken by you or your assistant, or even by an older child—some four-year-olds are kind and efficient at this sort of mothering. Keep the spare garments in an accessible place,

K

preferably near the washroom. A box for underpants, a box for trousers, a box for knickers, etc., will save a lot of time hunting through a pile of miscellaneous garments. Near at hand, keep a notebook with pencil attached to record the loan of clothes, and see that the entry is crossed out when they are returned. Also near at hand, keep a few clothes pegs, with a stock of slips of paper so that when a child's clothes are hung up to dry, his name can be pegged on, thus avoiding confusion later. With your spare clothes you will need to keep a few jerseys of different sizes, one or two dresses or skirts, some long trousers for the winter, and some pairs of socks. Shoes can conveniently be kept in a holder, each pair in its own pocket. Plastic shoebags can be bought quite cheaply, but as they are not very durable it is cheaper in the long run to make a suitable bag from some strong material. It should not be necessary to buy clothes, as mothers are usually glad to give you outgrown garments, but do see that these are not torn or crumpled, that all the buttons are on, and that the knicker elastic is effective.

One of the commonest causes of wet garments is over-enthusiastic waterplay, so make sure that you have sufficient aprons of a satisfactory type. You will also need aprons for messy activities like painting, working with clay, and finger-painting. Suggestions for making these will be found in the Appendix.

When children first come to nursery school, explain to them and their mothers about the 'protective clothing' provided and encourage its use. Sometimes a new child is distressed at the thought of wearing an apron; you can then excuse him temporarily, saying, 'You may play without an apron today, if you will be very careful, and tomorrow, when you are used to school, I'm sure you will want to wear one like the others'. Some mothers 'dress up' their children, particularly little girls, and then forbid them to get dirty in the sand or at the painting. In such a case sympathise with the mother in her desire to have the child looking nice, but explain the need for every child to feel free to join in without too much anxiety, and suggest that either she comes to school in her less precious dresses, or that her mother provides her with an overall to wear at school. There are, of course, some occasions when a child is being 'taken out' straight from school and so needs to keep reasonably clean: do your best to co-operate.

Preparation of Materials

A great deal of time can be saved by preparation of materials in bulk. When you prepare the powder paints, mix a good-sized jarful of each colour, and put a little into the jars that the children use; you can then afford to tip away any paint that has lost its fresh clear colour, and can easily replenish the jars if any colours are used up during the session. Dirty jars partly full of watery mud-coloured paint should never be tolerated. Ordinary jam-jars, or medium-sized Instant Coffee jars are a convenient size for the stocks of mixed paint, though this depends a little on the quantities used by the children. Remember to thicken the paint with a little cellulose paste, and not with cold water paste which does not keep well; in hot weather you will need to mix smaller quantities as certain colours soon begin to smell unpleasant. Keep your stock of mixed paint on a shelf near the sink, so that you quickly rinse the brush and jar before re-filling.

The paste used by the children for their creative work can also be mixed in bulk, if you use a cellulose paste. This is a great time-saver; the granules need a lot of stirring before they are completely dissolved and you can mix a large quantity as quickly as a small. Keep the stock jar handy, only putting a spoonful or so into the individual jars so that if they are knocked over there is not so much spilled.

The various kinds of paper used—newsprint, sugar paper, pastel paper, etc.—need to be cut into suitable sizes and various shapes. If you give half an hour to this once a week, you can prepare a good supply to draw on as necessary. This is much quicker than trying to do a few sheets before each session. Keep a suitable knife in some *safe* place, where the children cannot reach it, so that you do not waste time looking for it, or trying to cut the paper with scissors—a very long job, not to be undertaken unless you are cutting circles, etc. The various papers supplied for the college work can also be cut and stored in bulk, and a little put out at a time.

When you are planning each session, make a note of the items you must prepare in advance, and see that they are all to hand before the children come. This includes having your record-player and stock of records ready, the music books and percussion instruments at hand, your chosen story memorised or the picture book put ready, cookery ingredients collected, and so on. When the children arrive you will then be free to welcome them and to help them get busy immediately without any waiting around, though however carefully you plan, you must always be ready to cope with the unexpected. A child may arrive with a badly-grazed knee, requiring immediate first-aid and comforting, or with a doll Auntie has brought home from a holiday abroad, or with an urgent need to 'sew a present' for Grandma's birthday, or with a promise from his mother that *you* will supply the boxes for him to make the model castle which was the occasion of the storm, traces of whose tears can still be seen on his face. The answer to these unexpected demands is sensible storage and documented filing.

To take the storage first. Helped by your nursery assistant, keep your cupboards tidy, with a recognised place for each item, so that you can lay your hand on it immediately. Paper very easily becomes messy, so keep your larger cut-up pieces in a neat pile, colours together, so that you can see at a glance what you need, and also which needs replenishing. Smaller pieces of paper for collage work, etc. can conveniently be kept in cardboard boxes obtained from the local draper; these will stack neatly and can be labelled with their contents. If you have acquired a wallpaper book, ask a handyman father to take it to pieces for you—these books are very securely put together—and you will then have a neat pile of varied papers, instead of an untidy pile with torn ends. Whilst you do not want the children to expect only rectangular paper, it shows a lack of care to provide pieces that are carelessly torn, though if they tear their own, that is a different matter! If possible, keep a stock of cardboard with the paper: you can get this free by asking for boxes from the local shops and using the tops and bottoms; you may also be able to get some from the local hospital, as it is used for packing the X-ray films.

In the same cupboard as your paper, etc., keep scissors, Sellotape, paste, string, paper-fasteners—all the items needed for the creative table. Have distinctive containers for each item, and put out only a small quantity at a time. Six pairs of scissors should be plenty: remember to count them when you are clearing up as they are easily thrown away with waste paper. Stand pencils and felt-tip pens points up in a cylindrical container, or in a wooden block drilled with holes the correct size. Keep a pencil-sharpener near the pencils. A polythene bag is useful for collage materials: the children can then easily see what is available, but make certain the bag is not large enough to go over a child's head, as this is very dangerous and must never be allowed. A selection of pieces for collage can be put out in a tray on the creative table, and the rest kept readily accessible in the cupboard. Material for sewing is better kept in a basket or box, so that it does not get too crumpled. Keep alongside a box for sewing-thread and another for wool, each containing a tin of needles the correct size—packets are too easily mislaid. A couple of pairs of scissors sharp enough for cutting material can conveniently be kept with the sewing.

You will want to build up a collection of table toys from which a selection can be made each day. Keep them together on a shelf, making sure that each is complete before it is put away at the end of the day. The children will quickly learn to be careful about this, if you encourage them, and the older ones should be trusted to put equipment away at the end of the session.

A special shelf or bookrack should be available in the playroom for reference books. You need to be able to say to a child 'Let's look in the Atlas and see just where Stephen has gone for his holidays', or, 'If we look in the flower book we may find a picture of these flowers that Debbie picked on the way to school'. Keep these books where the children can reach them, then, when you are busy with something else you can send a child to fetch the required one. It is surprising how quickly they learn to find the right one.

You must also try to find room for the folder in which you file your pictures. Sort them into subjects—transport, countryside, foreign countries, people at work, etc., and let the children see any new ones and help you decide into which category they fit. They will also enjoy helping you find an appropriate illustration for a subject under discussion.

When you are planning your storage, try to arrange that the children have access to it and can help to put things away and to keep the shelves tidy. They should be free to take what they need, though they may be expected to tell you what they intend to do, so that you can check whether they are able to cope or whether they need help.

Putting things away, and keeping things tidy does not come naturally to children. With demonstration, help and praise they can learn to do so, but you must beware of overstressing this. On a school visit I watched a small boy laboriously pick up every scrap of paper under a table which had been used for cutting out. It took him nearly fifteen minutes and could have been done in two by an adult with a dustpan and brush. I regard this slave-labour as waste of a child's time.

Sweeping-up and mopping-up are often necessary. Ask for a long-handled broom that can be kept in a corner, and have a dustpan and brush hanging on a handy hook. A floorcloth should be available near the water-play, and a multi-purpose swab should hang by the sink: both these should be changed daily. Out of the children's reach hang a cloth kept solely for wiping lavatory floors, and within their reach put a small one for wiping wet lavatory seats. If a child vomits, sprinkle sawdust thickly on it; it can then be swept up easily. If paint or paste is spilled, see that it is wiped up immediately, or it will be trodden all over the room.

Finally, if you are having trouble with an activity, try to stand apart (metaphorically if not actually) and see what is wrong. Is your sand tray too full, so that it spills easily and sand gets all over the room? Or do you need to show more interest in the sand play and so discourage wild actions? Is your paint too runny, so that it drips from the painting as it is carried across the room? Do you need some new water-play apparatus to encourage more purposeful play and discourage splashing? Perhaps your room needs rearranging so that one activity does not clash with another. Perhaps you just have too much going on: you cannot do everything all the time! Rationalise your programme and your room arrangement, because nothing is gained from a messy environment where the children are unable to work, and the teacher is exhausted at the end of the day by her vain attempts to 'catch up'. A productive mess, a busy untidyness, does not matter; mere muddle should be avoided.

'Time Off'

In the full-day nursery school or class, where staff are with the children through the meal and rest periods, a short mid-morning break is desirable. This need not be more than ten minutes, fifteen at the outside, and certainly not the half-hour customary in some schools, and should be taken in the staffroom, where a brief rest is possible. Before you take your break, see that your assistant knows what to do—and do not expect her to supervise the room, put down the rest-beds, and wash up the paint pots, all while you drink your coffee! See that she also has time for her break. This brief period of relaxation should be regarded as a right, but one that you will both cheerfully forgo on a morning when, for some reason, everything has gone wrong. On the other hand, it *is* a right to which you are both entitled, and which will help you to cope better with the mid-day busyness. In a double-session school, on the other hand, where the children come for only two and a half or three hours, a coffee break is not only unnecessary, but takes up time that can ill be spared. You and your assistant must both be free, of course, to go around to the staff lavatory, but apart from this, you should spend all your time with the children. It is perfectly possible for your assistant to drink her coffee whilst supervising the children's milk, and for you to drink yours wherever you are working at the time, but do be careful that a hot drink is not put where a child could pull it over himself. I remember Barbara who pulled a cup of tea over herself at home. Months later she still flinched if her arm was touched for, although the scald had healed, her memory was still sensitive to the severe pain she had suffered.

Personal Possessions

Children's cloakroom pegs (and bathroom pegs in the full-time school) should be marked with a symbol and with the owner's name. A bag on each peg is useful for hats and scarves, but gloves should hang down coat sleeves on tape or elastic. The bags should be made of strong material, and may be supplied by the parents or by the school: they are easier for the children to manage if they are made on a small coathanger rather than with a draw-string at the top. Teach the children that everything they take off *must* be hung on their pegs or put in their bags, and not dropped on the floor, or even put in the dolls' wardrobe, which was where we found Gary's shoes one morning after a prolonged search. This is one of the few rules imposed at my school, and saves a great deal of time at the end of the session, especially in the hot weather, when the children strip down to their pants. In fact, any garment I find on the floor, I make the owner put on again, 'Or you won't know where it is at home time!'

In the playroom you will need a Treasure Box, where children can put the things they bring with them if they are not using them in their play. A large painted tin is satisfactory, or a plastic waste paper tub. It should be understood that the Treasure Box contains private property and not toys for general use, though a request to the owner that someone may 'have a go' may be all that is needed.

Staff also have private property that must be respected! Your handbag, your special books, your records should have a cupboard, or at any rate, a shelf of their own to which the children do not have free access, and, of course, this goes for your assistant as well.

And now we have reached the end of the book. You have arrived early at school, worked hard with the children all through the day, stayed at the end of the afternoon to clear up; you have given an evening a week to making equipment; you have even adopted my suggestions! What more can you do? Just this: you will be a better teacher if you have interests apart from your work, some intellectual, creative, social activities that enable you to take a more balanced view of your job. And as for those days when everything goes wrong—they happen to us all from time to time, and should not be occasions for undue anxiety, but rather for doing something interesting in the evening and following it with a good night's sleep. Take your work seriously but not solemnly—and I hope you enjoy it as much as I do.

Appendix

Waterplay aprons made with a thin absorbent towelling front are better than those with a smooth surface which allows the water to run down on to the child's shoes and socks. They are easy to make by putting the plastic and the towelling right sides together and stitching the top and sides, leaving the bottom open for turning. They should be long enough to reach to the child's knees, wide enough to wrap round his hips, and high enough to come well up under his chin. Stitch a length of webbing or wide tape to the shoulders so that if forms a loop hanging to the waist at the back. Stitch two more lengths to the sides, making these long enough to cross at the back, one string passing through the neck loop, and then to tie at the front; the child can then take off his own apron, though I have yet to find a really satisfactory one that he can put on unaided, for it must fit snugly to prevent water getting under it. Teach the children to come to you to have their aprons tied so that you can make sure they are well protected and their sleeves rolled up securely.

Small children may get wet even when wearing an apron if the water tray is rather high for them so that they have to lift their arms so high that the water runs up them. It may be possible to give them a box to stand on but it is a good idea to have a few aprons with short raglan sleeves, elastic cuffs, and a drawstring to tie at the neck. Be careful that the sleeves are not too tight and that the neck is comfortable, because plastic when gathered can be very sharp. If you have a handicapped child in your group these coveralls will be a necessity.

At the end of the session spread the aprons out to dry where the plastic will not be ruined on hot water pipes or the fireguard.

Aprons for painting and clay work can be a simple tabard style, i.e. two rectangles of material joined at the shoulders with straps and just below waist level with wide elastic. Alternatively a one-piece shape can be cut and the neck finished with binding. These aprons are the same back and front and can be managed unaided by all but the youngest children. A strong multi-coloured cotton is best; two sizes will be necessary, made in different colours to distinguish them, and do not forget loops of a contrasting colour to hang them up by. Make plenty of these, as they will need to be changed frequently for washing.

Finger-painting aprons can be made very cheaply from plastic sheeting. Strengthen the edges by turning them in over tape and then machining, using a long stitch and a loose tension. Put a neck loop as on the water-play aprons, but use one long piece of tape for the side strings, carrying it across the wrong side of the apron, and stitching it at the sides so that the length of tape between the stitching is slightly less than the width of the apron at this point, thus ensuring that the pull comes on the strings and not on the plastic sheeting. In order to protect the children's clothes when they are sitting down, cut the aprons rather wider than those you make for water-play, and make a dart each side at waist level, so that they fit better. Shorter strings that tie at the back will not get so messy with paste and paint.

Time spent on making these aprons will save a lot of labour during the session.

A Short Bibliography

Ash, B., Winn, A., Hutchinson, K.: Discovering with Young Children, *Elek*
(This has ideas for very many valuable pre-school activities, with suggestions of ways to get the most out of them.)

Axline, V.: Dibs in Search of Self, *Penguin*
(A very readable account of how a young child was helped, through play therapy, to come to terms with his problems.)

Fraiberg, S.: The Magic Years, *Methuen*
(She shares with the reader her insight into the behaviour of young children.)

Hartley, R., Frank, L., Goldenson, R.: Understanding Children's Play, *Routledge and Kegan Paul*
(Published twenty years ago, this is still the best book I know on nursery school play.)

Isaacs, S.: Social Development in Young Children, *Routledge and Kegan Paul*
(All those working with pre-school children should read Susan Isaacs.)

Jameson, K.: Pre-School and Infant Art, *Studio Vista*
(Excellent on the development of children's drawing, etc.)

Newson, J. & E.: Four Years Old in an Urban Community, *Allen and Unwin*
(Very interesting on home backgrounds and ideas on child-rearing.)

Pickard, P. M.: The Psychology of Developing Children, *Longman*
(Readable psychology and a very full bibliography.)

Willsher, B.: Call Me Person, *Pergamon*
(A delightful book about nursery school children, who sound nearly as nice as mine!)

Index

Aggression **89-92, 133-134**
  against an adult 90
           children 91
           inanimate objects 90
  frequent 91
  'might is right' 133
  outlets for 34, 89
  toddlers 133
  your attitude to 90, 92, 133
Aprons **144-145**
  clay-painting 145
  finger-painting 145
  waterplay 11, 144
Arranging the room **3-5**
  child's eye view 5
  creating corners 3
  display 4
  positioning of activities 3
  preparation 3, 138

Babies 47, 63, 132
Balloons 47
Bible stories 64, 101, 102
Biting **92-93,** 134
Bodies 47
Books **51-55**
  book list 54-55
  categories 51-52
  choosing books 51
  maintenance 53
  presentation & storage 52-53, 139
  science 49-50
  sources 53-54

Bricks **12-13**
  new interests 13
  siting 3
  storage 12-13
  supplementary material 13
  types 12, 30
Bubbles 47
Buffet services 78

Care of equipment
  books 53
  bricks 122
  brushes 16
  children helping 4, 19, 122
  clay 14
  home corner 19, 122
  outside toys 38, 40
  paint 16, 137
  sand 10, 40
  table toys 32, 33
  traffic toys 34
Caretaker 123
Christmas 64, 102
Clay **14-15**
  aprons 145
  care of 14
  supplementary materials 14
  working with 14-15
Clearing up
  after dinner 79-80
         milk 80
         play 7, 14, 15, 26, 33, 37
  outdoors 41

Control of the group 113–114
Cooking **35-37**
  eating 37
  in an oven 36
  on a ring 35–36
  preparation 36
  safety 35
  supervision 37
  techniques 36–37
  'uncooked cooking' 35
Creative table **20-24**
  adhesives 21
  'junk' 21–22
  presentation of materials 21–22
  taking work home 23
  teaching techniques 20
  three-dimensional work 21
  two-dimensional work 23
  variety of materials 20–21
Cuddling 59, 88
Deafness 60
Death 134
Dependent mothers 88
Display **4-5, 43-44**
  backgrounds for 44
Disturbed children 71, 100
Domestic staff 123
Dough **34-35**
  how to make 34
  semi-permanent 35
  supplementary materials 35
Drawing 23–24
Dressing-up 19
Electricity 48–49
Experimenting 12, 20, 27, 47
Fairy stories 63
Family tables 76–78
Feeding problems 126–127
Finger-painting **24-27**
  alternative method 26

aprons 145
clearing-up 26
handprints 26–27
making the paste 24–25
organisation 24–25
taking prints 26
Finger-plays 6, 7, 55, 67
Floor play 4
Flowers 5, 43, 46
Food allergies 79
Fragile treasures 44
Free activity 6–8
Fungi 46
Gardening 40
Gradual entry 85–87
Head teacher 119
Hearing test 60
Helping parents 88-89, 126–134
Home corner **17-19**
  construction 17
  crockery and cutlery 18
  dolls 18
  dressing-up 19
  'food' 18, 35
  furniture 18
  tidiness 19
Homegoing 7, 86, 88, 114–115
Hostility 134
House plants 46
How to make
  aprons 144–145
  bricks 12
  carpeting 18
  containers 4, 9, 11, 13, 14, 32, 43
  dough 34–35
  home corner 17
  home corner furniture 18
  musical instruments 69
Hymns 101–102
Illustrations 43, 44, 51, 52, 65, 139

Jealousy 91

Keeping one jump ahead 91, 135

Kitchen staff 122–123

Language **56-62, 103-110**
  arising from brick play 13
        cooking 37
        mealtimes 77
        outdoor play 39
        sand play 10
        traffic toys 34
  assessment 106–110
  assessment check list 107, 108–110
  correction 106
  development of 60–61
  enrichment 107
  expansion 61
  grammar 61, 103, 105
  kits 103
  rhythms of speech 105
  vocabulary 56, 57, 61, 65

Late children 115, 127

'Let your lives speak' 102

Livestock 44–45

Magic of wishing 94–95

Magnets 47

Medical staff 123–124
  inspections 123–124

Mid-day meal 76-80

Mid-session milk: 80–81

Mirrors 48

Music and movement 6, 7, **68-75**
  collecting material 74–75
  instruments 69–70
  music corner 68–69
  organised provision 72
  spontaneous groups 70–71

Naughtiness 93–94

Nursery assistant
  attitude to 119
  role of 121–122
  supervision 117
  working with 120

Nursery rhymes 52, 55, 60, 71

Nursery student 117–118

Outdoor play 6, 9, 10, 38–41

Over-dependent children 87–88

Painting 15–17, 23–24

Parents' problems 126–134

Personal possessions
  children's clothes 142
        treasures 111, 142
  staff property 142

Poetry 56, 57, 67

Prayers 101–102

Pre-maths 36, 99

Preparing
  paint 137
  paper 137
  paste 137

Printing 27–28

Priorities 135

'Productive mess' 141

Rain 47

Reading 98

Reference books 53, 139

Rejecting mothers 89

Rest **81-84**
  rest beds 83
  wet rest beds 83

Reverence for life 101

Role of the nursery assistant 121-2
        teacher 111–115

Rubbings 27

Rules 10, 31, 38, 112–113

Safety
  broken glass 17, 135
  cooking 36
  electricity 49, 113, 117
  eyes 10

Safety—*cont.*
  food allergies 79
  knives 117, 137
  outdoors 38, 112–113
  poisonous berries 46
  potential dangers 117
  rules 112–113
  woodwork 31
Sanctions 113
Sand **9–11,** 40
Saying sorry 92
Scientific interests **46–50**
  arising from clay 15
        cooking 37
        water-play 11–12
        weather 46–47
Scissors 22, 28, 87
Sensitivity 23, 100
Sewing 28–29
Sex instruction 132–133
Shyness 133
Singing 69, 71, 73
Sleeping problems **127-130**
  difficulty in
  getting to sleep 128–129
  late bedtime 127
  nightmares 129
  non-sleeping children 130
Spare clothing 136
Spiritual growth 100
Stammering 61
Storytime 6, 7, **62**
Storytelling **62-66**
  choice of story 63–65
  seating arrangements 64
  telling 65–66

Storage
  convenience 4, 137
  filing 43
  improvised 4, 43
  spare clothing 136
Students 124–125
Supervision 38, **116-117**
Swearing 96
Table toys 32–34
Tale-telling 95–96
Teaching moment 99
      points 68
      practice 125
Telling the truth 94–95
Temperature 49
Textures 27, 31
Threats 93
Tidiness 19, 140
'Time off' 141
Toilet training **130-131,** 135
Traffic toys 34
'Trying it on' 93
Turning a blind eye 92
Visiting pets 45
Visitors 119, 124
Water play **11-12,** 40
Weather charts 46
Wheeled toys 19, 39–40
Wind 46
Withdrawn children 59–60
Woodwork **30-31**
  tools 30
  wood 30
Writing 98, 99
Welcoming children 100, 111
      parents 111